Shifting Paradigms
Reshaping the Future of Industry

Dave Garwood and Michael Bane

R. D. Garwood, Inc.
PO Box 28755
Atlanta, GA 30358-0755
(800) 241-6653

Shifting Paradigms:
Reshaping the Future of Industry

© 1990, Dogwood Publishing Company, Inc.
501 Village Trace, Building 9A
Marietta, GA 30067

"40-Hour Week," © MCA Music

First Printing, October 1990
Second Printing, April 1991
Third Printing, March 1992

ISBN 0-9621118-5-6

This R.D. Garwood, Inc. publication
is printed on recycled paper.

Design and graphics
by McShane & Moore Associates

We would like to personally recognize and thank a long list of truly outstanding individuals. Each has made a tremendous contribution to every page of this book.

We have always been fortunate to have a long list of clients who serve, at times, as laboratories for new ideas and concepts. The most rewarding aspect of our business is the opportunity to build strong personal and professional relationships with the leaders of these outstanding companies. Unfortunately, space does not allow us to acknowledge each individual by name, and for that, we apologize.

Among the individuals who were kind enough to review the manuscript and give us excellent feedback were Brian Kemp, Chief Executive, Simon Engineering; Charles Heineman, VP Manufacturing and Engineering, Ashbrook, Simon & Hartley; Don Bently, Chairman & CEO, Bently Nevada; Roger Harker, President, Bently Nevada; Dave Biggs, VP Manufacturing and Product Development, Bently Nevada; Bruce Achenbach, Vice President, Trane Company; Joe Beebe, VP Operations, Intermec Corporation; Jim Lyness, Business Analysis Consultant, Eastman Kodak; Greg Mahoney, Development Engineer, Eastman Kodak; Jim Teegarden, Group VP Support Services, Fisher Controls; Craig Anderson, Manager Materials, Fisher Controls; and private investor Lee Saunders. And special recognition to Dave Biggs, who has become a pioneer in the new product development process. That chapter largely reflects Dave's ideas.

We are also blessed with the opportunity to work closely with other leading professionals in the field. Phil Crosby was kind enough to take time from his busy schedule to give us his invaluable critique. David Buker shared his experiences with us and provided valuable information.

We feel privileged to also have an opportunity to work with an outstanding group of individuals...our Excellence Team. In particular, John Civerolo, Chris

III

Gray, Bob Jones and Bob Stahl, spent many hours pouring over the manuscript and helped straighten out our thinking at times.

In many ways, the words in this book are a compilation of the thoughts, experiences and convictions of these fine people and several others who were not mentioned. We are deeply indebted to each.

Numerous other people have made outstanding contributions in their own right. Our entire office staff— Bob Donehew, Marian Rosswaag, Barbara Van Horn, Phyllis Byerly and Marilyn Parker—helped enormously in coordinating a long list of activities necessary to put this book together. We especially want to thank Mary Ellen Moore and Andrea Morton for their editing.

Finally, a special recognition to Lynn Garwood. Not only did she contribute to making the book readable, but her patience during the periods of frustration and delay provided the support we needed to get the job done.

FOREWORD

I met Dave Garwood under unusual circumstances. I was working in my office and the phone rang. I answered it, and a deep voice on the other end said, "Hello, my name is Dave Garwood."

That doesn't sound unusual, and it wasn't up to that point. But then Dave asked me if he could get my permission to use the phrase "Shifting Paradigms" as part of the title of his new book. That was unusual.

I told Dave I didn't own the words, that he could title his book anything he wanted. And still he insisted that I be comfortable with his use of words that I had, through my video, "The Business Of Paradigms," brought into common use in business.

A man of fair play and respect, I thought to myself.

And since that phone call, I have continued to discover in Dave Garwood those kinds of positive attributes. He cares deeply about people and their abilities to succeed in a highly competitive world. He believes that if you treat people right, give them the right kind of education, that they can be the base of success for any company. And that is why he is so committed to the Total Quality Movement.

I have spent a fair amount of time listening to many consultants talk about their approaches to Total Quality. I admire all of them, but Dave Garwood, for me, has always made the most sense. He combines the best discipline with a working knowledge of making Total Quality happen on the shop floors and couples that with his natural teaching skills and humor. Heck of a combination.

The book he has written with Michael Bane and which you are about to read is important in the field of Total Quality. It deals with the basic question of why the adoption of Total Quality is so important. It delivers its message clearly—a compliment I wish I could give more books on quality. It has examples that make sense and illustrate the leverage of the new paradigm. It has humor, which I believe is an important measure of maturity of Dave's understanding of the whole process.

And yet it is not a cookbook on Quality. It is, rather, the justification, the proof, for why you should do all the real work that is necessary to make your organization ready to compete in the coming years.

When asked to identify the most important paradigm shift of the 20th Century, I always say Total Quality. Not the collapse of Communism; not the introduction of biotechnology. Total Quality wins because it has proven that it can effect positively every aspect of life, from the products we use to the services we require. From the shape of our own jobs to the success of our nations.

I believe that the base of the 21st Century is predicated on TQM. And because of that, any business, any organization, any nation that doesn't practice Total Quality in some for cannot be competitive. TQM will be the new separator between the haves and the have-nots. Those that practice Total Quality, organizations and nations, will move rapidly toward what could only be described by a 20th Century person as "Utopia." Those who do not get on board will be left to a more and more distant second place—not caused by lack of resources or technology, but simply lack of application of the Total Quality process. It will be that simple and that important.

Several years ago, in an essay, I suggested that, "Without caring, there can be no quality." It is clear that Dave and Michael care deeply about the Quality Revolution. I think this book will make you care, too.

And it is under the banner of Total Quality that I want to thank Dave and Michael for writing this book. It is a great way to begin your exploration of and, hopefully, your commitment to the movement.

May your pathway lead you to excellence, which will lead you to success!

Joel Arthur Barker
Author
Future Edge

How to use this book

Shifting Paradigms is designed not just to read, but to use.

We've designed a step-by-step path for achieving World Class performance standards. Each step, we feel, requires a wholesale change in mindset, a paradigm shift, to truly succeed.

First, we've isolated the traditional paradigms, showing how those paradigms have crippled our productivity. Then we've outlined the new paradigms, and how your company can make the move. Almost every chapter begins with a story, the adventures of the fictional company Feel Good, Inc. The chapters end with Discussion Points, helping you to apply the points of each chapter to your own company.

To use the book:

1. Each member of your Executive Team should read one chapter at a time.

2. The Executive Team meets to review how the chapter's topic applies to your company and to discuss how to apply the principles.

3. Establish an action plan.

4. Act!

Think of *Shifting Paradigms* as an Executive Summary. *The Facilitator's Guide* is also available to guide you through the steps (see our order form in the back of the book). *The Guide* picks up where the Discussion Points leave off, providing a chapter-by-chapter breakdown of how to gain the benefits of the new paradigm.

We've set up an easy-to-follow format that will help you swing your own "Silent Majority" over to the side of change.

Best of all, the *Shifting Paradigms* program works! Our program has been refined in more than 20 years of teaching and consulting with such companies as Coca-Cola, Eastman Kodak, Georgia Pacific, GTE and the many companies mentioned in *Shifting Paradigms*.

It's not enough to want to change; to be discontented with the present. We feel strongly that there has to be a path, a way for change to succeed. We hope you'll join us on this path.

Shifting Paradigms:
Reshaping the Future of Industry

False Starts And Wild Punches

The war is over, and we think we won.

At least, that's the message we see again and again in the business press, hear over lunches in swank business waterholes and executive boardrooms. We have met the challenge of global competition, and we have triumphed.

And the facts seem to back up that happy analysis. America's largest manufacturers enjoyed their most prosperous year in recent history during the late 1980s. *Fortune* magazine reported that USA factories and refineries were operating at "near capacity," with Fortune 500 sales topping $2 trillion for the first time ever. All around the world the business climate seems to be changing. Eastern Europe is in the throes of *perestroika* while western Europe digests the European Economic Community.

Sure, we had the tough decade of the 1980s, nearly got clobbered by the Japanese and the Pacific Rim, but American industry on the whole is finally back on track, ready to take on the world. It's as though we can all heave a sigh of relief and get on with the important business of making money. America's CEOs, for the first time in decades, are breathing more easily, feeling comfortable that they can compete.

But is that really the case?

Has the Great American Industrial Machine come through the battle, ready to get on with business as usual?

We think not.

In fact, we think American industry is facing its biggest challenge since World War II, a challenge that will see it either emerge once again as the preeminent world manufacturing power or fall so far behind that it will look back fondly on the dark days of the mid-1970s.

American industry is at a critical juncture, with critical decisions to be made. Those decisions aren't about capital spending for automation, recabling the factory for new computer-integrated manufacturing, hammering the unions for wage concessions or opening a new assembly plant in the Yucatan.

The critical decisions industry faces go deeper than the day-to-day running of the business, all the way to the basic decisions, the basic approaches to how we run our businesses.

And it doesn't matter whether we're in the business of manufacturing cars or chemicals, whether we're a small machine shop or General Motors. We're all affected.

The question for the 1990s and beyond is this: *Are we willing to run our businesses differently?*

In 1974, futurist Joel Arthur Barker began talking about the concept of *paradigms*. Paradigms, as described by Barker, are the templates, the shared assumptions, we use to look at our world. Barker's definition of paradigms reads like this:

"A paradigm is a set of rules and regulations that 1) defines boundaries, and 2) tells you what to do to be successful within those boundaries. Success is measured by the problems you solve using those rules and regulations."

Basically, paradigms are the glasses—the assumptions and beliefs, the filters—through which we see our world.

Basically, paradigms are the glasses—the assumptions and beliefs, the filters—through which we see our world. And they are amazingly powerful. An example Barker uses is one from recent history. Remember, in the 1960s, the incredibly vicious battles over the length of men's hair? Families literally broke up over the question of, "What was manly?" In the 1980s, where male sex symbols run the gamut from bald to long pony tails hair-wise, the whole battle seems silly and a bit childish. In the 1960s, it was neither. Instead, it was a reflection of the existing paradigm—and the new paradigm that was challenging it.

Let's look at manufacturing. Did you know, for

example, that the digital watch, the ubiquitous time-piece that has driven the finely tuned Swiss product off the market, was originally invented by none other than the Swiss themselves? A fact. Yet the Swiss, who, at that time, 1967, dominated the watch market, drastically underestimated the effect of the digital watch, not even bothering to protect their own invention.

The Swiss didn't see the world-shaking implications of their own invention, because, according to their existing paradigm, watches had mainsprings and ticked. Watches had hands and faces. Even the electronic quartz watch met those criteria. The Swiss' existing paradigm served as *blinders*, blinding them to the ramifications of their own invention. Other similar examples abound; it's not even hard to think of examples close to home.

And there is a difference between what we might consider an intellectual paradigm and a practical paradigm—what we say we do and what we really do.

We have certain paradigms on how we think we're *supposed* to run a manufacturing business, and the way we *really* do it. We're comfortable with those paradigms. It may be the way we've always run our businesses, or it may just be "good common sense." Direct labor efficiency was important, wasn't it? Workers worked; management did the thinking. As the first efficiency expert, Frederick W. Taylor, said at the turn of the century, "Under our system, a worker is told just what to do and how to do it. Any improvement he makes upon the orders given him is fatal to his success."

That view of the worker shaped policy and practices for decades. Is it any surprise that the labor union movement took root so quickly and grew strong?

We saw inventory as an asset; suppliers as enemies. Engineering designed new products; manufacturing figured out how to make them.

But while we're working within the old paradigm, we're blind to change sneaking up on us. Even more important, we're blind to the opportunities that shifting paradigms can bring us. Look at the Japanese auto industry, still riding a positive wave generated by shifting paradigms, away from the "accepted" thinking

3

of low gas mileage and planned obsolescence to high mileage and high quality.

Are we willing to challenge the basic assumptions on which we run our businesses; shift our paradigms of how to run a manufacturing business?

If we're not, our efforts to reach World Class performance standards are doomed to fail. If we insist on doing more of the same, we can expect more of the same results. We're not talking here about refining our process, tweaking or fine-tuning old practices. We're not talking pockets of excellence in businesses. Instead, we are talking about a baseline change, a paradigm shift. And if we can't make that shift, we are going to see our late 1980s' industrial renaissance vanish like so much smoke.

But what are the new paradigms, the World Class standards? If our business is profitable and competitive today, doesn't that mean we're World Class? Haven't a number of companies even adopted the theme of World Class manufacturing in their marketing efforts?

Smoke and mirrors aside, what we are talking about is achieving the highest levels of performance in areas of quality, cost reductions and flexibility to customer needs. The very best companies are just beginning to touch those standards. And those standards are a moving target.

"Consumers," said former President Ronald Reagan, "by seeking quality and value, set the standards of acceptability for products and services by 'voting' with their marketplace dollars, rewarding efficient producers of better quality products and performance."

The operative words here are better quality and performance.

"World Class quality means providing products and services that meet customer needs and expectations," says Donald Peterson, former CEO of Ford Motor Company, "at a cost that represents value to the customer."

Perhaps the ultimate test of a World Class organization is its focus on continuously getting better, what Japanese managers refer to as, "many small ways of doing things a little better."

> **If we insist on doing more of the same, we can expect more of the same results.**

"From a retrospective point of view," says James W. Teegarden, group vice president for Fisher Controls, "we thought we were good three to five years ago. Had we not continued to improve our performance, we would not even be considered competitive today."

In our 20 years of working with some of the top companies in industry, we've seen the high bar consistently *rise*, meaning we have to work even harder. Let's look at a sports analogy. Remember Roger Bannister? A few years ago, Roger Bannister ran a mile in four minutes. A four-minute mile! A new world class standard! It seemed incredible—Roger Bannister's story was on television and in the newspapers, and we shook our heads in awe at the achievement.

Suppose you run a four-minute mile today. Will your name be up in lights and shouted by sports commentators? Of course not. Run a four-minute mile today, and you might get a ribbon at a high school track meet. Anything wrong with Roger Bannister? No, of course not. At the time he ran the four-minute mile, that was the standard, the world class level of excellence. But the standard for excellence hasn't stood still.

In fact, the high bar has risen. We're able to achieve more now than we ever would have believed possible just a few short years ago.

Just a few years back, we played on a small track— competing locally, regionally or even nationally. And we had winning times. But a winning time in a local track meet doesn't necessarily qualify you for the big leagues. In fact, think of how that winning local time stacks up in a world-size playing field, the Olympics. Today's global market is the equivalent of the Olympics. A time that was good enough to sweep the state championships might not even be close enough for a shot at the Olympics. And what happens at each Olympic competition?

Times get faster. The competition gets tougher.

The lessons we can learn from the Olympics are simple: With a bigger playing field and more players, there are more *good* players. And, as we learn more about competing, competition gets tougher. There are

5

not nearly as many runaway successes that totally dominate a market. Instead, as one CEO recently put it, manufacturing has become a game of inches, being a little ahead of the competition most of the time.

And that means steadily getting better. What was good enough in the past may not cut it today and surely won't cut it tomorrow.

The problem, of course, is that we've looked everywhere for improvement except at the basics of running our businesses. We've methodically attacked the symptoms with a variety of patent-medicine acronyms from MRP II to CIM while the disease ran on unchecked.

And what is the disease?

Low quality. High costs. Slow response.

An inability to respond quickly to shifts in product mix or to changing market conditions. Slow time to market for new products. Institutionalized inefficiencies that led us to the next major problem:

A lousy bottom line.

How did we get to this impasse?

Let's look, briefly, across the ocean at the Japanese. There's a feeling among some manufacturing CEOs that the Japanese played a dirty trick on us by building high-quality products, forcing us to play catch-up. That isn't what happened, though. The Japanese, mostly through desperation, adopted a new paradigm, a new view of the world. It had to do with quality, of course, but it had to do with much more, including cost reductions, organization, responsibility and many other factors. The Japanese suspected it would be more efficient and cheaper to make the product right the first time around.

We in America didn't start out with the intent of making low-quality products. Nobody's business plan included making shoddy merchandise and pawning it off on an unsuspecting public. Nor did we intend to set up manufacturing systems that maximized the cost of producing our product or that was slow to respond to the needs of the marketplace. We always *intended* to be high-quality, low-cost, fast-response producers. And by our old standards, the old paradigm, we did suc-

Manufacturing has become a game of inches.

6

ceed—and may still be succeeding—for a while. But we were not facing reality.

With the best of intentions, we deployed tactics that resulted in the opposite of what we wanted. We eliminated workers instead of work, leaving an over-worked workforce in shell shock.

We invested heavily in technology—hardware, computers, automation. In fact, our very performance measurement systems—the way we judged whether we were doing good or doing bad—actually contributed to many of our problems. By our own standards, we could be doing excellently and still be dying in the market-place—the ultimate performance measurement! That's exactly what happened in the automobile and small electronics industry, where we thought we were doing just fine until we were run over by people who didn't use our personal yardsticks, our paradigm. We even institutionalized our inefficiencies and waste, called them "standards," and judged ourselves on how well we met them!

Our myopia was, perhaps, understandable.

The American postwar manufacturing machine was an awesome beast. The manufacturing power that had produced literally incredible amounts of war materials was now turned on the booming consumer market. The new consumers, after years of deprivation, had money in their pockets and hard goods on their minds. Houses, cars, appliances, the new category of consumer electronics, clothing, furniture—the list seemed endless, and the market could go nowhere but up.

From our 1950s viewpoint, it was a fairly contented market. They bought what we made—because it was new, because it was blue, because the Joneses bought one, because it had bigger tail fins. No matter, the market was growing, incomes and leisure time were on the rise, and there was no reason to imagine that it wouldn't go on forever. The market was capacity-driven—you make it, and we can sell it.

By the 1960s, that complacency had filtered into our manufacturing strategies. Of course, the customers would buy whatever we made. They always had, hadn't

We even institutionalized our inefficiencies and waste, called them standards.

7

they? The focus on manufacturing in the 1960s was on producing more to service an ever-growing market.

That situation might have gone on forever if it hadn't been for a couple of monsters rattling around the closet.

In 1974, we ran out of gas—literally. The gasoline crisis of the mid-1970s catapulted the gas-stingy Japanese car into the public view and literally overnight redefined the whole concept of "Made In Japan," another paradigm shift.

Japan didn't play by the rules!

It gave the customer what the customer wanted.

Japanese cars didn't get just a little better gas mileage than their American counterparts—they got a lot better gas mileage!

Japan didn't play by the rules!

And guess what? Instead of junk on wheels, we discovered finely made, high-quality precision machines. The Japanese were quick learners—you probably don't remember the first tiny Honda. By the mid-1970s, even the bottom-of-the-line Toyota was of higher quality than some top-of-the-line American sedans. The doors closed! The trim didn't peel off after two months! Even the radio sounded good!

At the same time, the enormously powerful Japanese personal electronics industry began a renewed assault on the American market. Sony's brilliant marketing, coupled with its undeniably superior product, helped bring home the realization that quality, performance and innovation came from overseas.

The effect on American manufacturing was devastating.

The complacency of the 1960s had given us a paradigm, a mindset that the customer bought what we produced, and we, as the producers, knew what was best for those customers.

The result was nothing short of shock. Words like "Rust Belt" and "apocalypse" began being heard in executive retreats. Confusion reigned. We entered a period of thumbsucking.

Were we really okay, just playing on an uneven field? After all, those other guys got low wages and government subsidies. Maybe the grass really was greener on the other side of the sea. Were we, in fact, finished as a world industrial power? Should we shift our national emphasis to service industries and let our factories relocate off-shore?

Should we emulate or invade Japan? Sing company songs and eat more raw fish? Or was the problem even worse than we feared? Maybe our workers had forgotten the work ethic. The pride was going, going, maybe already gone. Or maybe we should ask the government to build Fortress America with a new bout of protectionism.

"Japan is number one (in industrial productivity)," wrote John Naisbitt in *MegaTrends*, the 1982 book that perhaps best summed up our period of industrial angst. "But that is like a new world champion in a declining sport. It is too late to recapture our industrial supremacy because we are no longer an industrial economy...We must put down our old industrial tasks and pick up the tasks of the future."

The new tasks of the future were *service* tasks, providing services for the coming Third World industrial powerhouses. We were going through the birthing throes of the "Information Society," the death of the Industrial Revolution. What was left of American industry would no doubt be converted to a "lights-out" environment:

"Quality robots that cost $50,000 each can each work two shifts a day for eight years," Naisbitt wrote in *MegaTrends*. "That figures out to about $5 per hour—quite a bit less than an auto worker's $15 per hour salary and benefits."

But what about the Post-Industrial Society? Could we survive in a society where everybody, as one pundit put it, carried everybody else's luggage?

No.

"To live well," concluded the landmark MIT study on productivity, "a nation must produce well." Manufacturing, the production of goods, was inextricably linked to our standard of living.

There were other voices of agreement, some even from our competitors: "You can't survive with just a service industry," said Tsutomu Ohshima, senior man-

9

aging director of Toyota Motor Corporation.

With our rusting, non-automated factories and our cocky across-the-ocean competitors, we were clearly on the ropes, almost down for the count. And like the proverbial fighter against the ropes, we began striking out with wild punches and false starts, looking for the unseen force that was going to save us.

Talk about wild punches! Automation—there was a big straw. If we could automate everything, recable the company from the ground up, get those $5 per hour robots cranking away, maybe we could pull ourselves off the mat. "Automate or evaporate!" briefly became the slogan of the hour. Of course, automation *was* cripplingly expensive, and some of our accountants were warning us that we could never pay off the automation debt even if we dominated our market.

Well, maybe if we couldn't get those $5 per hour robots in place, we could beat our workers down to $5 per hour. Wage concessions and union bashing was right up there with automation as a way out of our dilemma. After all, we reasoned, the secret of our offshore competitors was the low labor cost. We neatly closed our eyes to the high labor costs in Japan, our chief nemesis, blinked away the undeniable fact that direct labor accounts for only a small percentage of the costs of our products, and called for wage concessions or even wage rollbacks.

Concessions and rollbacks were seen as a smart idea as long as it wasn't our own wages being rolled back. Of course, we were methodically destroying the morale of our work force, making ourselves an even greater enemy than Japan.

What the heck—ship the whole thing off-shore. If the Pacific Rim can make products so cheaply, maybe we should move our production facilities over there. *Outsourcing*, which sounded much better than *capitulating*, was a popular wild punch. Along with the production facilities, though, went American jobs and even more American money. Plus, just because we moved the factory off-shore didn't mean our customers would buy the product. We also ran the huge risk of exporting our knowledge and technology in addition to our factories, a reverse brain-drain that can—and has—led to the off-shore operations suddenly wondering why they needed us anyway. *Business Week* called it the "hollow corporation," no manufacturing, just selling and distributing, and they painted a glum picture.

"American companies have either shifted output to low-wage countries or come to buy parts and assembled products from countries like Japan that can make quality products at low prices," observed Akio Morita, chairman and co-founder of Sony Corporation. "The result is a hollowing of American industry. The United States is abandoning its status as an industrial power."

Pretty soon, it looked like there was nothing left to do but call in the cavalry in the form of government regulations, protective tariffs, wage and price controls and the whole plethora of protectionism. But once caught in the government quagmire, it is hard—if not impossible—to get out. Nor did government guarantees translate into increased sales. The situation looked even worse—if computers, robots, friendly unions and the U.S. government couldn't save us, who could?

When all else fails, reorganize.

Upstairs, we threw another wild punch. Let's "reorganize" our way to the front of the race! Because of our concern for quality and for overseas competitiveness, we first added a Vice President of Productivity, then a Vice President of Quality, then a Vice President of Japanese Ideas, all with appropriate staffs. Later, we added a Vice President of Robots, as we were considering floating a stock option to raise a few hundred million to retool and recable the plant. We moved a lot of boxes around on the flow chart.

The operative plan became find the good idea, budget it, staff it, then replace it with the next good idea. Whether it was MRP II, JIT, Computer Integrated Manufacturing or Quality Circles, we tried it all.

The pain refused to go away. So we tried to sell it off.

Companies like B.F. Goodrich, which had begun its life as a tire company, was no longer a tire company. It focused primarily on chemicals and plastics, products with better profit margins than tires. General Electric abandoned televisions for more lucrative fields. While gross size shrunk, profits soared. But products that had been produced, and produced successfully, in America were no longer made by American-owned companies.

In the early 1980s, just as the hand-wringing and chest-beating was reaching a crescendo, a strange thing started happening. Some of the wild punches started to connect.

The fact was American industry was filled with fat, the result of two decades of unchallenged industrial supremacy. In a desperate effort to streamline industry, American business leaders began attacking the largest areas of fat, the $20-million problems. Plant closings, factory consolidations, lay-offs, mergers and across-the-board budget cuts marked what was to become a period of restructuring, "meat-axe management." Focus turned to activities that could be accomplished by just a few people.

Companies began paring down their product lines, reorganizing their management teams, spinning off marginally profitable divisions.

It was time to trim down to fighting weight.

Growth, which had been the virtual religion of the 1960s, came into question. Maybe being the biggest wasn't necessarily the best.

Against all odds, American industry began lifting itself off the ropes.

But it wasn't enough.

What we did was mortgage our future in search of short-term bottom line results. Strategically, moving out of traditional markets made short-term economic sense. But short-term thinking was part of the reason we were in the fix we were in. It was the manufacturing equivalent of selling off the seed corn.

Slowly, though, we began discovering the secret of the Japanese. Not just the quick fixes, either. No two-week Japanese factory tours with enlightenment as part of the package.

I remember on my first trip to Japan, I was ready.

The fact was American industry was filled with fat.

I'd read all the articles about the new space-age Japanese factories, lights-out, no people, just robots and computers. I took a flashlight in case I went on a plant tour, so I'd be able to look around. I was shocked to discover factories full of people, working. The Japanese secret wasn't automation. Nor was it factory uniforms, company songs, quality circles, kanban, or any of the other *techniques* that panicky American businesses brought back from the Far East.

The Japanese had rediscovered something simpler, something we had long taken for granted—the customer.

Who hands out the blue ribbons in the competitive race, anyway? The customers!

But American industry had forgotten that simple fact. Remember, we *told* the customer what they should buy—this year's model, in blue. We didn't *ask*, not really. And even when we did make the effort to ask, the communications channels between the customer and management were clogged with decades of bureaucracy. And when we did ask, we asked the wrong questions, trapped in specifics—would you prefer red or blue, when we should have been asking, *What do you really want?* What do you *expect* from the product, from your supplier, from your workers, from your management? Do they meet your expectations?

The global competition ushered in by the 1974 oil embargo, which produced visible lines for gasoline, gave consumers a choice they hadn't previously had. The global competitors raised customers' expectations.

And despite a built-in predilection to "buy American," American consumers opted to buy quality.

We have learned some bitter lessons about paradigms. The classic example is General Motors, which decided to build cars the Japanese way. But GM looked at the Japanese way and perceived that the secrets were automation, new high-tech factories and all the bells and whistles associated with the old paradigm.

After a $70 billion spending spree, GM discovered a startling fact: At its NUMMI plant in California, a joint venture between GM and Toyota, managers were

American consumers opted to buy quality.

achieving Japanese-like results *without* all the bells and whistles. In fact, Toyota opted for less sophisticated machinery just so it could train American workers in the Toyota way of making cars.

"For those who believed that the Japanese industrial edge rested solely on technological prowess, the NUMMI experiment was a real revelation," wrote industry analyst Maryann Keller in her 1989 book on GM, *Rude Awakening*. "The Toyota secret was, finally, no secret at all. Treat both white and blue collar workers with respect, encourage them to think independently, allow them to make decisions and make them feel connected to an important effort. Combine that culture with a good car and quality parts, and the results are obvious."

Which prompted H. Ross Perot, at one time embroiled with GM, to quip, "Brains and wits will beat capital spending ten times out of ten."

Ironically, Ford Motor Company, unable to afford the staggering tab for automation, dug in and took a serious look at the way they made cars.

"Our approach has been that there are times when technology isn't the best answer," said Ford spokesman Jay Meisenhelder. "Maybe just reorganizing the way you do things can work just as well."

The results?

By 1986 Ford was little more than half the size of GM, but nearly twice as profitable.

That's the power of shifting paradigms. And it doesn't matter whether we're talking about the giants of the automobile industry or the smallest mom-and-pop shop. The power of the paradigm shift remains.

We have not, in fact, turned into a service economy. There's now some doubt as to whether such a change is ever likely to happen, and, should it happen, whether it's really the panacea its proponents have envisioned.

"The strength of this dominant view—that the American economic future is assured by a smooth shift into services—is based on data that, (while) overwhelming in their seeming consistency and scope, to a large extent reflect a statistical muddle," wrote Stephen

S. Cohen and John Zysman in their book, *Manufacturing Matters: The Myth Of The Post-Industrial Society*. "Shift out of manufacturing and it is more likely that you will find that you have shifted out of such services as product and process engineering, than into those services."

Instead of the ultimate service economy, with everyone carrying everyone else's luggage, we offer new paradigms, paradigms for the continued resurgence of manufacturing.

The basis of the new paradigm is simple: To paraphrase *A Quality Revolution* commentator Colin Seidor, "Listen to the two groups of people who count—the ones who make the product, and the ones who buy the product."

And here's how to make sure their voices are heard.

15

DISCUSSION POINTS

1) Discuss what shifting paradigms means. How does it apply to your business?

2) Identify key indicators, such as market share, customer satisfaction and profits, and discuss how your improvements in these areas stack up against your competitors.

3) Identify a couple of existing paradigms in your business and discuss how you would like to see them change.

4) What fundamental changes in how you run your business have been made in the last two years? Discuss them.

5) Discuss the "quick fixes" described in this chapter. How many have you tried?

Business As Usual

Quality.

Makes sense, doesn't it?

When we buy a shirt, we expect both sleeves to be the same color. When we take an aspirin, we expect our headache to subside. When we hire someone to clean the house, we expect the house to be cleaner than when we left it. We expect our car doors to close, our CD players to produce good sound, our air conditioners to cool us off.

In short, we, as consumers—customers—expect a quality product or service when we lay down our hard-earned bucks.

But what, exactly, is quality?

That's a more difficult question to answer than you might expect. Yet it's a question we *must* answer before we can compete and make a profit.

The classic definition of quality, as articulated by Phil Crosby, is *conformance to requirements*. The widget works. The doors close. The stereo plays. All the buttons are on the shirt.

A quality product is one that meets 100 percent of its requirements 100 percent of the time. If we say this is a 500 milligram dose, and we weigh the pill, it should be 500 milligrams.

Could it be 499 milligrams and still be considered a quality product?

That totally depends on the requirements. If we defined the requirements for that particular pill as 500 milligrams, plus or minus 10 milligrams, 499 milligrams would be perfectly acceptable.

Consider this story.

It's Saturday morning and you're running late. One kid needs to be dropped off at soccer practice; the other has a piano lesson. Both are at noon, on opposite ends of town. And, of course, don't forget to cash a check, pick up the dry cleaning, get some propane for tonight's barbecue and the car needs oil and a lube job. Before everything closes at 3 p.m.

By 1:30, only half the tasks are done, and you're starving. No problem—that's why fast food restaurants were created. You spot a burger palace, pull in and order the "standard product"—cheeseburger, fries and a chocolate milkshake—no specials, skip the escargot. After you pull forward and pay $12.75—hardly a bargain—the young woman at the window tells you to pull over by the jungle gym and park!

"Sorry. We got a large order just before you arrived," says the employee at the window, noting that sales had failed to forecast it. "School bus full of band members just came through and cleaned out the cheeseburger inventory. Not to worry; we're thawing out more meat."

And you thought this was fast food!

When you finally get your food, you don't even open the sack you're in such a hurry. At the first stoplight you reach into the sack and—guess what?—no fries. You might not know it, but this particular burger palace just received the annual quality award. They implemented Statistical Process Control (SPC), tracked the temperature of the fries, and it never varied more than one-half of one degree either way. You're not impressed. The fries are not in your sack!

A bite of the cheeseburger reveals no cheese. You'd have really enjoyed that cheese, though, since the quality has been flawless for three years. The burger place has the x-bar charts to prove it.

Enough is enough. You head back to the burger palace to register your complaints. The clerk, though, has an unexpected response: "Are you *sure* you didn't eat those fries?"

I give up! The french fry bandit caught at last!

The quality of the product may be outstanding, but, as a customer, you're unimpressed. In fact, they've just received your lowest quality rating, even though by their own measurements, the quality is excellent, even World Class. The food from the burger palace met all the requirements as outlined by the undeniably high standards of the corporate office—precise temperature control, fresh foods, a standardization of portion size.

But let's go back to our initial discussion of quality. We *expect* both sleeves of our shirt to be the same color. We *expect* our car doors to close, our stereo to play music, our aspirin to work. The key word here is *expect*. A true definition of quality is rooted in customer expectations.

What our burger palace overlooked—what many American businesses have traditionally overlooked— is that the only quality evaluation that really counts is measured through the eyes of the customer—not the engineers, not the line workers, not the inspectors. And customers expect more than just a product that works. Customers expect to receive what they order. They expect to have it delivered when they need it. And they don't expect a lot of hassle.

Quality, then, can be defined as *conformance to expectations*, and those expectations must come from the customer. That's the same customer who, for years, remember, we've taken for granted. If we want to play on the global ball field, that has to change. Global competition requires World Class performance to win. To achieve that performance, we have to understand and accept the concept of a customer focus, a customer-driven business.

The implications of a customer-driven business represent nothing short of a revolution for many companies. Two of the most important of those implications include:

-Manufacturing as a team event. In order to make the steady, small improvements we need to stay ahead, we're going to need everyone in the company pulling together.

-The necessary common mission. When everyone pulls together, they need to be pulling in the same direction. Our Mission is to perform to World Class standards, as high-quality, low-cost, fast-response producers, and that's the direction we all need to be traveling in.

When we talk about quality with a capital "Q,"

The only quality evaluation that really counts is measured through the eyes of the customer.

quality in a World Class sense, those are the kinds of issues we have to address. Yet, generally, when we talk about quality, we find ourselves trapped in the narrow confines of product quality, adroitly avoiding the forest by concentrating on all those trees.

One of the other things we notice about focusing on product quality, quality with a small "Q," is that it has led us to some erroneous conclusions about why things don't work, conclusions that reflect the old paradigm. When we think of poor product quality, whose fault is it? Remember the old joke about "Friday cars," cars built on Friday when all the workers wanted to go home for the weekend? If you got a car built on Friday, forget about the doors closing or the air conditioner working. The joke reinforced something we all felt: *Workers* were responsible for poor product quality. Those guys on the line screwed up and our television sets only receive two channels. The reason our Sonys worked was because Japanese workers were more conscientious than their American counterparts.

See how well that concept floats down at the local bar after work!

Not only was it an insulting concept that the American worker was only marginally human, it was wrong. Research by Dr. Edwards W. Deming—a national treasure in Japan and only recently recognized in his home country—on quality problems had turned up some interesting statistics. In statistical analyses of quality problems, Deming found that the overwhelming majority of quality problems were caused by circumstances over which the worker had no control! In fact, worker-caused quality problems amounted to less than 10 percent of the overall number.

What about the other 90 percent?

Well, if the workers didn't cause the problems, management must have. We adroitly shifted from worker-bashing to management-bashing. During the period of false starts and wild punches, one of the most persistent cries heard was that the American style of management was seemingly responsible for everything from quality problems to the common cold.

Yet once the fur stopped flying, we discovered

that American managers were doing exactly what their Japanese counterparts were doing—managing according to a specified set of rules. The old paradigm effectively restricted our vision.

The root of our quality problems, the root of our industrial malaise, was neither our workers nor our management.

Instead, *our problems were rooted in the way we had chosen to run our businesses.* The problems were not with the players; the problems were with the rules, the old paradigms. Bad processes, not bad people!

With the best of intentions, we evolved a way of doing business that gave us results exactly the opposite of what we intended. Or, as manufacturing consultant David Buker says, "We were chasing the wrong rabbits."

Take, for example, unions. Unions arose to combat a valid problem, the exploitation of the work force by management. The tools used to accomplish unionization's goals included rigid job classifications, strict adherence to seniority rights and, in general, a very strict, very hierarchic bureaucratic structure. As we move into a customer-driven market, however, one of our key competitive elements is flexibility, speed. In Japan, for example, quality is a given, the ante to get into the game. *Everyone's* door closes! The widgets all work. So what is the key competitive element?

Flexibility.

How quickly can you respond to a shift in the market? How quickly can you change your product mix or bring a critical new product to market?

To be World Class is to be able to respond quickly. A part of that quick response is being able to make full use of our most valuable resource, our people, when and where we need them. Yet strict job classifications and a rigid hierarchy work against us. The old paradigm—us versus them—simply will not work.

Quality? Of course we were concerned with quality, which is why we set up a rigorous series of inspections—a whole department dedicated to Quality Assurance, in fact. Quality Assurance sorted the good ones from the bad ones. The good ones got sent to the customers, while the bad ones sat around until the end

The old paradigm was to correct, not prevent, defects.

of the month, when they miraculously turned into good ones and got shipped anyway. Our "quality" efforts, then, were really "sorting" efforts. The old paradigm was to correct, not prevent, defects.

What that series of inspections didn't do was attack the causes of the quality problem in the first place. Instead, we accepted—even institutionalized—poor quality and tried to compensate for it. We called the compensation factors the yield or scrap factor, and we got very good at predicting yields, making all the proper allowances, setting aside a portion of our capacity for reworking scrap parts. We gave *good* inspection; why wasn't our quality going up?

We became, in fact, World Class at the wrong things.

About the only thing going up were the costs—costs for inspectors and inspection equipment, costs for scrap, costs for rework. Phil Crosby includes these in the "cost of quality," and estimates as much as 25 percent or more of the revenue is spent correcting what should have been done right the first time! Try as we might, we couldn't inspect quality in.

When we tried to take an overall look at how we were doing, all the indicators said, "Great." All our indicators led us to believe the system was working. We became, in fact, World Class at the wrong things.

The old paradigm for Purchasing was simple: Focus on price and lower it. Produce a favorable price variance, usually by hammering our vendors. A five percent favorable purchase price variance was good for a raise, or at least continued employment.

But how did that really work? What really happened?

We established a standard price for purchased material—bolts, for example—told our Purchasing Manager to "get it as cheap as you can." Our Purchasing Manager knows that if he orders one bolt, it's $1. If he orders 100 bolts, it's 99 cents apiece...until pretty soon he's reasoned out that buying a warehouse full of bolts is the best way to "get it as cheap as you can."

But we only needed 1,000 bolts a year. And Engineering was working on a design modification that will obsolete the bolt next month. But those favorable price variances looked good on the reports.

Meanwhile, on the plant floor, we had all sorts of good things going on. The plant floor had its own rules and boundaries, established by years of tradition. For a start, the machines were running, 24 hours a day, seven days a week. Which was good, since those suckers cost big bucks. In fact, we used machine utilization as a way of measuring how well things were going on the shop floor. If the machines were running 100 percent of the time, things were going great, best case. We installed a machine that could produce three-month's worth of subwidgets in an incredible 30 minutes! By the end of the first day's morning shift, with 100 percent utilization, we had enough subwidgets for four years! At the end of the week, we began plans for another high-rise warehouse.

We were also vitally concerned with worker efficiency, driving down direct labor costs. If we could produce a more efficient worker, we could make more money. So we commissioned a major time and motion study. Men in ties with stopwatches and clipboards were everywhere, breaking down each job into infinitesimal steps, clocking everything. We'd gotten good at time and motion studies. We could tell you to the hundredth of a second how long a task took, on the average, and with a little computer work, we were able to put stop-start indicators at every workstation, allowing us to compare actual time to do the job with the standard time allowed. Of course, the floor supervisors no longer had time to supervise; they needed all their time for explaining those variances! Many people were busier reporting than producing.

Or we brought in labor-cutting consultants, who evicted everyone who wasn't moving—heaven forbid they should be thinking on the job! We confused motion with productivity.

Besides, as we've mentioned, direct labor makes up less than 10 percent of our product's cost, and the percentage of direct labor in product cost was and had been steadily shrinking since the turn of the century.

Our cost-accounting systems, originally derived primarily to value inventory for tax purposes and for external reporting requirements, found it convenient to base the allocation of all non-direct or overhead expenses on direct labor. The ratio of indirect to direct could be 10 to 1, which led us down the primrose path of believing that reducing $1 of direct labor actually reduced costs by $11. These "facts" were even used to justify capital expenditures and calculate gross margins. Pricing, product pruning, capital investments, deployment of resources and a host of other decisions were based on this shaky data.

With the old paradigm blinders on, everything looked rosy.

The time and motion studies also told us that the best way to arrange our factories was functionally—all the drill presses in one place, all the printing presses in another. It was more efficient. Unfortunately, it also broke the bond between worker and product—Daddy could no longer quite explain to his children what he did at work, since "driving five screws into the left-hand inside door panel," didn't have quite the appeal of "building fast cars."

And we did those things, the wrong things, well. We turned determining the Economic Order Quantity (EOQ) into a finely tuned science. We created high-speed, state-of-the-art quantitative analysis. We became masters of the time and motion study. We became very good at building high-rise, automated warehouses. We sic'ed newly minted B-school MBAs on every problem in sight. Quantitative analysis became the method of choice for getting at the "right" answers. With the old paradigm blinders on, everything looked rosy.

The important thing to remember is that none of these ideas were bad ideas. None of them were scurrilous attempts to produce low quality, high cost goods. Each effort was aimed at producing higher quality, lower cost goods, better servicing our customers. People weren't bad, incapable or lazy—just misguided.

Our problem was not a question of doing things right; instead, it was a question of doing the right things!

We drew up the rules, the way we ran our businesses, and then we measured ourselves against those rules. We scored great. Let's take a look at reality, the results of all the old paradigms at work:

TRADITIONAL FLOW

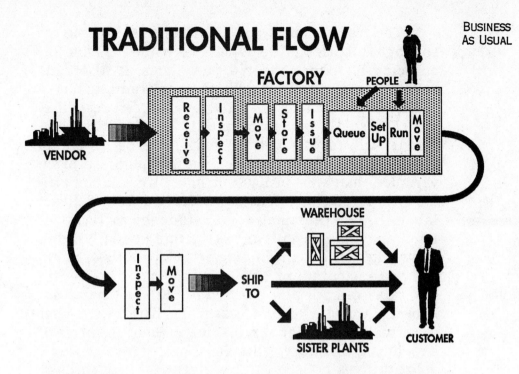

This is a graphic representation of the traditional way we've run our businesses, a snapshot, if you will, of the ugly truth. Now that we have that snapshot, let's develop it:

Material arrives from the supplier. We receive it, inspect it, store it, eventually issue it—hopefully before it's obsolete or lost! Once issued to the plant floor, it waits in queue (Q). Eventually, the equipment is changed over—or set-up—(SU), the item is run (R) and moved (M) to the next operation. The steps can be duplicated many times until the product is completed. Once finished, the product is shipped to the customer, warehouses or a sister plant.

When we look at this traditional process, what do we see?

For a start, it takes time to get through the process. Say we're having quality problems in the product that's being shipped. By the time we communicate those problems back down through the chain, the people who did the original work might not even still be employed there! There are lots of steps here adding *cost* but not *value*. Each inspection, storage, movement, queue means more dollars lost.

The traditional process is today's reality, the result of the series of decisions we made—maybe unconsciously—under the old paradigms. It also runs counter to our Mission statement—performing to World Class standards in high-quality, low-cost, fast-response.

We tried to maintain quality by inspection and compensate for the loss of it by factoring in scrap/yield. We measured performance by purchase price variance, machine utilization and direct labor efficiency. We sought to cut down the amount of direct labor through automation. We thought in terms of functional plant layouts and EOQs, and we really didn't know whether our inventory records or bills of material were accurate or not—and they weren't. We did our sales planning in a vacuum, the right hand not knowing what the left hand was doing. When we thought in terms of customer service, we thought in terms of expediting, an informal system of personal follow-ups, substitutions, hot lists and red tags to push through what we really needed; purchasing or making a little bit extra of everything to cover up the lack of good planning. Finally, we take all the inefficiencies and pass them on as price increases to the customers. For a long time, "inflation" was a convenient excuse. We call this "business as usual."

Recently, we received a resume from a very impressive graduate interested in getting into manufacturing. In addition to his substantial academic credits, he'd had a summer internship with a Fortune 500 manufacturing company (who shall remain nameless here for obvious reasons). His job there had been, "...working from departmental shortage lists to locate misplaced and lost material."

We institutionalized the BandAid solution, then we taught this promising young person that jury-rigging was normal! When he finally breaks into manufacturing, the thing he's going to remember most from his exposure to one of the largest manufacturing companies in America is that you've got to be sure to have someone out there looking for the lost stuff, which must be as inevitable as death and taxes. We helped shape the wrong paradigm!

We institutionalized the BandAid solution.

A recent article in *Inc.* magazine offered suggestions for dealing with year-end "inventory write-downs," the way we explain to our auditors about all that lost stuff. Instead of taking a single painful hit at the end of the fiscal year, why not divide the write-down by 12 and factor it in for each month? That way, the stuff's still lost, but the books still balance perfectly at the end of the year and the pain is spread out. The writer went on to gush about how well the system had worked at his company. The books were always balanced.

And it all worked. We got product out the door, even if we had to disassemble some other product to do it. The traditional ways of running our business, with its attendant informal systems and hidden agendas, will work, but with a critical proviso—*traditional ways only work in low-competition or monopolistic situations.* In a high-competition situation, where the customer has a large number of choices, the company that most satisfies that customer wins.

What we're going to suggest is that we do something a little radical, something a materials manager told us: Do as little as possible, but what you must do, do 100 percent right, 100 percent of the time. We want to eliminate the unnecessary activities, move as many activities from the "necessary" column to the "unnecessary" column, then eliminate them.

In fact, we'd like to move to the ideal manufacturing process—raw material arrives in the morning, finished product ships out in the afternoon. We make only as much as we need; not as much as we can.

Let's look at a diagram of the ideal process, a vision of the new paradigm:

IDEAL FLOW

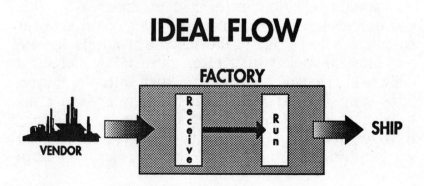

What's one of the first things we can eliminate to get us closer to the ideal process? Let's focus on storage. We've got high-rise warehouses the size of Cleveland and more being built. Why do we have the storage in the first place?

It turns out there are lots of reasons.

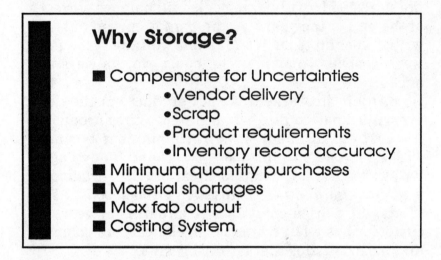

Why Storage?

■ Compensate for Uncertainties
  • Vendor delivery
  • Scrap
  • Product requirements
  • Inventory record accuracy
■ Minimum quantity purchases
■ Material shortages
■ Max fab output
■ Costing System

Obviously, we can't just bring in the bulldozers and knock down a couple of warehouses. The first thing we're going to have to do is address all those uncertainties. The first thing you'll notice is that those uncertainties aren't just confined to the factory floor or Engineering. Everybody in the company is going to have to participate in making these uncertainties go away. To meet our customers' expectations, then, everyone in the company has to pitch in—it's a company problem, not a Manufacturing problem.

Look at the other items affecting storage. EOQs and price breaks—buy a million, and we'll get a two percent price break.

Maximum output in each department...Why? Because that's the way it's done, isn't it? Make as many as we can, and we're making the best use of our machinery.

More than anything else, we're talking about a change in mindset, another paradigm shift. Computerizing is not the answer, although computers are going to be necessary to help us make the change. We may have to put a robot here or there or automate some of the handling. We may have to put some equipment in place to efficiently collect data we have to have. We may have to rethink our production processes, make sure our inventory records are accurate, retrain our people to feel comfortable with minimum inventory. But all these things are only *part* of the overall solution.

They are not the solution!

You'll notice that the true "costs" of storage are hidden throughout the balance sheet and income statement. On the Balance Sheet, under plant and equipment, we have the costs of our automated storage and retrieval system and the numerous forklifts we use to shuffle boxes. Hidden in Receivables are products that are never going to get paid for—because we sent the customer the wrong item from our inventory or the product we sent doesn't work. Long-Term Debt includes our new highly automated high-rise warehouse to store the unnecessary inventory.

On the Income Statement, some of the costs of storage are lumped under that old devil Overhead. There's also storage cost hidden in Material Cost, R&D and SG&A as transactions to keep track of the units and dollars as materials are moved in and out of storage areas. The cost of storage is all over the board! An old friend, the late Joe Orlicky, called it the "Cost of Confusion."

Hand-in-hand with the quick fix mentality is the sense that there's a single huge problem, and if we could just solve that big sucker everything would work out well. If we could just wave our hand and solve the "Storage Problem." This is a major problem for many companies. Executives *understand* solving problems; the bigger the problem, the better. Unfortunately, there's no single huge problem to be solved. Look at storage, caused by hundreds, even thousands of problems. Just as the costs are all over the board, so are the solutions. The same goes for queue, inspection, and so forth.

Remember the "meat axe" restructurings? Those restructurings focused on the $20-million problems and could be accomplished by three people—the CEO, a lawyer and an investment banker with a telephone. Sort of the Henry Kissinger "lone gunslinger" scenario. But now the situation is different. There's no $20-mil-

Unfortunately, there's no single huge problem to be solved.

lion problem lurking on the shop floor. Instead, there's a million $20-problems. Each of those problems might be very easy to fix. To solve those million $20-problems, we're going to need more than three people—a lot more. The challenge becomes how to lead people, make them *want* to solve those problems and then empower them to solve the problems without bogging them down in miles of red tape!

Problems that by themselves are small potatoes. But small problems add up. A million small problems make a mountain.

If we honestly look at our operation and see the myriad small problems, it becomes obvious that change is not a "Project," an activity with a clearly defined beginning and ending. Change is a constant process. Improvement is a constant process, a chipping away at that mountain of small problems. We think the American mindset wants to see those single big problems, then smash them to pieces with a single blow of a big sledgehammer. One blow erases all. The idea of steadily chipping away lacks the romantic appeal of that one decisive blow.

It is, however, the only way to succeed!

A customer focus is necessary for World Class performance, but is it enough?

Think for a moment about the Japanese electronic industry. They did more than meet their customers' expectations—they *raised* those expectations, met the higher expectation, then raised them again. Remote controls, stereo sound, even the rise of the CD are reflections of raised consumer expectations.

The only way to raise expectations—and then meet those raised expectations—is through continuous improvement. Business as usual just won't cut it anymore.

To summarize:

1) Total quality is the key, the umbrella under which all the other programs fall.

2) Traditional paradigms won't get you to World Class performance.

3) Focus on the Mission: Perform to World Class standards to become a high-quality, low-cost, highly flexible producer.

4) Shift to the new paradigms: Change how we run our businesses.

5) Concentrate on continuous, small improvements, a race with no finish line.

So the survival question is *how can we become World Class producers?* That's what *Shifting Paradigms* is all about. Each following chapter discusses a key element in the quest for performing to World Class standards.

What we hope to achieve is paradigm shifts in quality, new product development, supplier relationships, factory/plant floor operations, planning, organizational responsibilities, performance measurements and accounting systems.

Each chapter begins with the traditional paradigms, then moves forward with companies who have challenged those traditional assumptions and succeeded. Each chapter concludes with discussion points to help you apply the concepts to your company and get you moving on the right track. The final chapter concentrates on how to bring off the paradigm shifts.

What we're talking about is not that hard to grasp. We're not talking about inventing a new machine or getting the software up and running. Technology isn't where it's at. The real secret is mindset. Probably the hardest concept to grasp is that of *continuous improvement;* the idea of doing it all over again; the idea of *process* rather than *project.* It was Rod Canion, CEO of the enormously successful Compaq Computer Corp., who said manufacturing has become a game of inches, not miles. To succeed, we must be a little bit ahead most of the time, because it's unlikely we'll ever again have the huge lead we had once. Conversely, if you're behind, you can expect to catch up a little bit at a time, not through one giant step or a cosmic computer program.

You don't have to be a rocket scientist to understand the concepts. And some of the concepts are going to sound familiar. But, beyond common sense or common practice, we do need a change in mindset—a new view of the world.

The good news is that the battle is winnable, and we do have a plan.

The real secret is mindset.

31

DISCUSSION POINTS

1) Discuss what Total Quality means in your business.

2) What do your customers expect?

3) Look at the Traditional Flow diagram and discuss how it applies to your business. Which steps would you like to minimize, and what are the likely obstacles to overcome?

4) Identify three old paradigms, and discuss how they contribute to low quality, high cost and slow response.

5) Discuss specifically how the three old paradigms affect your income statement and balance sheet. Which items are affected, why and by how much?

CHAPTER 3

Is Quality Job One?

One Friday afternoon, all the executives and managers of Feel Good, Inc., makers of digital electronic analyzers and chemical solvents, had their first office party. The occasion for the party was Marketing's new graphs, which showed them with a 37 percent market share, up three points that quarter. Their nearest competitor in the fragmented market held only 18 percent.

The execs had another reason for celebrating—warranty claims were less than three percent.

"It darn well should be," said the Vice President of Manufacturing. "We've added two shifts of roving inspectors, plus increased the size of the QA Department by 26 percent. No defective analyzers or contaminated solvents get out the door!"

The VP of Engineering shrugged—the cost of doing business. He had other things on his mind; he'd seen some first-run products from a Korean factory—don't ask how they came into his hands!—and they were beauties. His own people had a couple of design ideas that would keep them competitive, but he was almost afraid to bring them up to the VP of Manufacturing.

"Look how badly we handled the last batch of Engineering changes!" Manufacturing had fumed. "We're already reworking 18 percent of the stuff and dumping one out of 10 batches of solvent. It's a damn miracle that we're delivering 50 percent on time."

The VP of Personnel could believe that. The company was losing a lot of top-notch people on the factory floor because the pace was just burning them up. It was expedite, expedite, expedite, and the orders

QUALITY

OLD PARADIGM

- Costly
- Inspect for Quality
- Product Quality Only
- Expensive = High Quality
- QA Job
- Always Some Defects

NEW PARADIGM

- Saves Money
- Do it Right the 1st Time
- Total Quality Expectations
- High Quality is Conformance to Expectations
- Everyone's Job
- Zero Defects

kept on coming. Making the shipping schedule at the end of each month was...exciting, to say the least. QA was always getting their arm twisted to accept, not reject. The order of the day was red-lined specs and substitutions.

One thing for sure, though, quality costs big bucks. He also shrugged—the cost of doing business.

The VP of Finance, the CEO's right-hand woman, was holding court in another part of the room. The cost of quality, she was explaining to a new batch of freshly minted MBAs, was clobbering the company.

"We gotta do it, though," she concluded. "Damn the competition!"

Sort the good ones from the bad ones.

Quality is expensive, right?

Higher quality means higher costs.

That is probably the single most pervasive assumption in American business, the very paradigm that the Japanese clobbered us over the head with. Remember back in the late 1960s? Of course, things were of poor quality. That was the point. They were expected to wear out—remember planned obsolescence? Quality was available, of course, but only at a (high) cost. And that was the way the world worked.

Or so we thought.

There are a whole series of corollary points to the main quality-is-expensive assumption:

1) The way to get high quality was through inspection; sort the good ones from the bad ones.

2) Quality applies primarily to the product; as we saw in the previous chapter, when we said we had poor quality, we meant the analyzer didn't work or the solvents weren't solvent enough.

3) We decided that the best way to deal with the quality problem was to institutionalize it, then predict it. This ends up with the apocryphal story of the manufacturer who demanded a 98 percent yield, that is, 98 percent good ones, from a supplier. The shipment of 1,000 arrived in two boxes. When the inspectors

poured over the boxes, they discovered that, in the big box, 980 of the parts were perfect; in the small box, the 20 remaining parts were defective. When the manufacturers called to demand what gives, the supplier just shrugged. "We didn't know why you needed 20 bad ones," the supplier said, "but we thought we'd put them in a separate box for you."

4) Quality was the responsibility of the Quality Assurance Department. Why else would they have that name?

5) Quality problems were created on the plant floor.

6) Problems with quality reflect poor attitudes or the lack of discipline of our workers, the ingrates. Obviously, craftsmanship and the work ethic were dead. This also conveniently exonerated management from any responsibility for quality problems.

All those assumptions in the traditional paradigm are based on common sense, aren't they? A custom-made dining room table costs more than a table the same size purchased off the floor of a discount store. A Saville Row suit costs more than the same gray pin-stripe from Acme Discount Clothing and Plumbing Supply. The items cost more because they're higher quality, right?

No, not at all. More hours might have gone into the custom furniture or the Saville Row suit, finer workmanship, more precision. But is that a proper reflection of quality?

Let's look at another example. Which is of higher quality, a stadium hotdog or a lobster dinner? Well, a lobster dinner might be really great, but if you're up in the stands watching Atlanta clobber the Mets, it's going to be awfully hard to hold the lobster in one hand. And if you're in the mood for soft lights, white wine and mood music, that hotdog with mustard, pickles and relish just doesn't cut it. The key here is customer expectations. Both the stadium hotdog and the lobster dinner can be high quality, depending on our expectations. A cheap dining room table may be just what we need for a summer house, and an off-the-rack suit might serve exactly the same purpose as the pricey Saville Row item. The key thing is that what we think of as

This also conveniently exonerated management from any responsibility for quality problems.

35

quality is not an absolute. Instead, it is related to the expectations of the customer. Costly does not necessarily equate with quality; nor does high quality mean high cost.

We assumed quality was expensive for a series of reasons:

1) We saw "quality" only in terms of product quality, whereas our customers saw quality as a series of items and events that included product quality, on-time delivery, perceived value for the money, etc. Our earlier definitions of quality, as a matter of fact, were all geared to product quality alone. Think about Crosby's conformance to requirements or quality guru Dr. J. M. Juran's "fitness for use" definition of quality. While neither intended these concepts to focus solely on the product—in fact, they emphatically stated the opposite—it was easy to misinterpret requirements and fitness as synonymous with specifications, which are product-oriented.

Our earlier definitions of quality. . .were all geared to product quality alone.

If we think of quality as tied to expectations, let's expand that definition throughout the factory. Let's take a person working on the plant floor. Who is that person's customer? Ultimately, of course, it's the consumer, the end-user. But isn't the next person in the production process also a customer? Doesn't the next person have a set of expectations? Those expectations might include that the material or subassembly or whatever be put together correctly or blended by the earlier workers, that it be delivered at the work station in a timely manner—not too soon, where the material will stack up, or too late, causing the line to bog down.

But there are other expectations as well. A line worker might expect that he or she be provided with the proper tools for the job, that the lighting and environment be correct for the kind of work being done, that safety requirements be met, that the recipe or specifications for mixing or building the product be correct, that the material going into the product not be faulty, that the correct diagrams or instructions for making the product be available, that an adequate amount of time be allocated to make the product and so on.

2) We thought the only way to get higher quality was a tighter inspection net, which was, in fact, expensive and non-value-adding to the product.

Our views on inspection are based on other, more painful assumptions:

The world is full of crooks, and they're called our employees and suppliers—right? They're making garbage and trying to palm the stuff off on the next guy, only we've got a policeman, an inspector, at the door and on the line who nails 'em.

3) We were guilty of first-degree over-design, demanding the "best" instead of what was necessary to do the job.

4) We often did not understand our customers' expectations, creating products that were technically or technologically superior, but not necessarily meeting our customers' needs.

5) Perhaps most important, we saw quality solely as an external function; that is, we thought of quality only in terms of things that affect the product, as seen through the eyes of our external customers—quality as a function of warranty claims, so to speak. While that is a part of what quality is, to be sure, it's only one part.

There have been reams written about the need for product quality, and we agree that, if the product doesn't work, your chance of winning the Competitive Race is slim indeed. But, in many ways, a strict focus on product quality leads us back into the trap Feel Good, Inc., found itself in. As we stated earlier, American industry has been trying to "inspect in" quality for decades—and it does work! Sort of. If you inspect every single outgoing item and only ship the good ones, you will have product quality in the customers' eyes. And huge amounts of rework. And a schedule that looks like World War III. And high costs, a demoralized work force, poor response time to the market and, in general, a company in a total "react" mode. It's the difference between prevention—actually solving the problems—and detecting the problems, then sorting out the good from the bad, after the fact.

The real question is whether the expectations of both the internal and external customer are clear. Do

We thought the only way to get higher quality was a tighter inspection net.

37

we understand the expectations of our customers? Are they clear?

Let's refocus for a few minutes on that last point. If we are truly looking for total quality—"Quality" with a capital "Q"—we must focus on the expectations of the internal customer as well as the external customer. We are all customers. If we imagine a factory with a traditional Henry Ford-type assembly line, every person on that line is the customer of the person before, or upstream of, him or her. What about the first person on the line? Well, that person is a customer of the vendors who supply the components or raw materials. Just like the external customer, the internal customer has a series of expectations. They might, for example, expect shop floor/plant schedules and supplier schedules to be valid. It's hard to deliver on time when red tags, hot lists, or shouting in the hallways provide the only answers to "What do we really need and when do we need it?"

The new paradigm for quality, the paradigm that's going to take the quality movement into the 1990s and beyond, looks like this:

1) An awareness of Quality with a Capital "Q." That is, we understand that quality is more than product quality; that it is, instead, meeting all of the expectations of both the external and internal customer. This definition of quality dovetails with our new focus on the people who buy the product and the people who make the product.

2) We see improved quality as minimizing variability, keeping in mind that we will always have variability in our processes and product. We want to strive, though, to continuously reduce that variability until it's well within accepted limits. The goal should be, to use Crosby's terminology, "Zero defects."

3) We think in terms of continuous improvement of processes and products. We want to eliminate the unnecessary tasks, the non-value-adding activities, then move as many necessary tasks into the unnecessary column as possible and eliminate them, too. We are aware that continuous improvement is a process itself—no beginning and no end.

Continuous improvement is a process itself—no beginning and no end.

38

4) We place the responsibility for quality at the source, not on a separate set of inspectors. In the past, we've thought of this primarily as making equipment operators responsible for the quality of their output, and that's correct. Responsibility at the source also means that management has the responsibility to correct those quality problems that fall under their venue—which is the majority of the problems! Inspection isn't totally eliminated—instead, it's transferred to the point where the work is originally done.

5) We understand the true cost of quality. We've always assumed that quality was expensive, while overlooking the actual cost-cutting benefits of a total quality program. The most significant benefits from a total quality program may be reductions in the "re's"— re-work, re-placement, re-counting, re-structuring, re-doing, re-issuing, re-scheduling, re-promising, re-typing. We are talking big numbers here. The big savings from a total quality program may well be from cost reductions, not just warranty claim reductions.

"...Continuous quality improvement does reduce costs," says James Teegarden of Fisher Controls. "It takes time, money and training and demonstrated management commitment, but continuous quality improvement does produce bottom line results."

Our old paradigm saw cost increases rising directly with increasing quality—a linear function. But, at some point, the savings that accumulate from avoiding doing the work to correct defects pays off. In fact, the graph of quality versus cost looks a little like Mt. Fuji, which is why the Japanese call it the "Mt. Fuji Effect."

In reality, it's low quality, not high quality, that's expensive.

Picking The Right Tools

The quality movement over the last few years has been important in introducing several problem-solving tools to the business world. None of these tools is new—we've used them, formally or informally, for years. We're talking about tools like run charts, brainstorming, cause/effect diagrams, pareto charts, control charts, team building, communication skills and facilitator skills.

Notice that these tools focus in two areas— finding out what the real problem, the root cause, is, then developing solutions. We're going to be referring back to these tools throughout the book. Communication skills are vital for the factory of the future. We want to have thousands of people trying to solve our million $20-problems—how are we going to understand what they're trying to tell us? Take, for instance, an enormously skilled old hand on the shop floor. We've spent 20 years telling this person to shut up and run the machine. Now we'd like this same person to tell us how to make the job better or more efficient. We're surprised when the person doesn't answer? We owe that person a chance to learn problem-solving and communications skills—it's an obligation on management's part. That's where the quality payoff comes from!

Some of those tools need a little more explanation. Statistical Process Control (SPC), for example, was on the way to becoming a confusing acronym in its own right. With SPC, we chart a process to see whether or not it's under control. We then work to bring the process under control and reduce that process' variability.

Variability is another dimension to quality. In a process, the more variability, the greater the potential for quality problems.

Let's look at a typical chart of results over time:

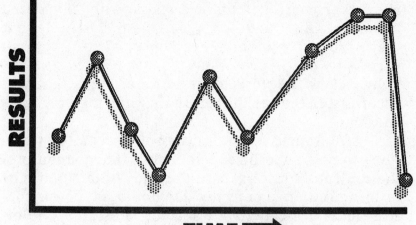

It doesn't matter if the results represent market share, earnings per share, on-time delivery, data quality or product quality. There are two elements to this graph. The first is whether we're performing at the level we want to be. The second is the question of variability. One thing is for certain: If we keep doing things the way we've been doing them, the level of performance and variability will stay the same—next week, next month, next year. That is, we get the same results.

The principles of variability are simple:

1) Identify the critical parameters and chart their performance. For example, if you're driving down a highway, the process of getting home, a critical parameter for safe driving is not the bass level on the stereo. Some critical parameters are air pressure in the tires, good steering and clear vision.

2) Bring the process under control first. One indication that a process is out of control is when too many data points are outside the upper or lower control limits. If too many data points occur near the limits, or if the trends run up or down or the process runs above or below average, the process may also be out of control. First, eliminate the surprises, data points well outside the limits. If extreme or too many data points occur outside the limits or are skewed above or below the mean, better find out why. The variation isn't

41

normal, and the surprise may be even bigger next time.

3) Understand tolerance versus limits. Upper and lower control limits are statistically calculated based on actual data—they may be undesirable, but they're fact. They identify the "normal" or expected variability of the process as it is currently operated. They tell us the percentage of data points that will occur inside the calculated limits when the process is "normal."

Tolerances are definitions of acceptable variation—they're imposed or established independently of the control limits. Any result outside of the tolerance is, by definition, a defect. When upper and lower control limits are calculated and fall outside the tolerances, the odds of having defects are quite high. We don't want to place tighter tolerances than necessary—that's over-engineering, which is partially responsible for getting us into this problem in the first place. At the same time, we want a process that will consistently produce material inside the tolerances.

> **We must focus our efforts on reducing that variation until all defects are eliminated.**

4) Minimize variation. This is an imperfect world, and we will always have some variation in our processes. However, we must focus our efforts on reducing that variation until all defects are eliminated. There's a cost issue as well. The costs to replace or re-do those items—whether it be material, inventory records, or schedules—that are outside acceptable limits, can be quite high.

5) Perform to expectations. While a process may be under statistical control, it is not necessarily performing at the expected level. We always have to keep going back to the internal and external customers, sort of a reality check. What are the expectations of the process? Are we meeting those expectations? If our car is always inside the yellow line and the edge of the road, but on the wrong side, look out! Statistically, the process is under control, but it's not where we want it to be. Good results, or zero defects, then mean we are consistently, 100 percent of the time, at the correct level of expectation, and the variation is within accepted limits.

We recently heard about a major American company that was getting clobbered by their competition—American, by the way. One of the most important items cited by the clobbered company's QA chief was the competition's ability to get SPC "up and running" because they had new software. His company's whole quality program was on "hold" while they waited for new hardware and software that would "allow" them to put a quality program in place.

Nonsense! SPC is not just charts and graphs. You can start using the principles of variability to help you understand your processes this afternoon. And it doesn't matter which equipment you have or process you choose. At Trane Company in Macon, Georgia, one team decided to use the principles of variability to analyze interoffice memos.

It worked, allowing the team to improve communications while reducing memos.

A Spicy Story

Here's a story about how one company solved its quality problems. One of our clients, Tone's, Inc., of Des Moines, is a spice company, which cleans, grinds, mixes and packages many different spices. The spice business is a tough one, especially when it comes to forecasting. In fact, because of the nature of the grocery business, Tone's realized its forecasts could never be as accurate as they liked. The way the company had previously compensated for forecast inaccuracies was to carry lots of inventory. Large runs of each kind of spice placed in inventory until needed supposedly kept costs down.

Of course, for a business that's been around since 1873, sometimes inventory got lost...or spilled...or spoiled...or just plain stacked up. Pretty soon, nobody knew what exactly was in inventory...just that there was a lot of it.

Forget where it was stored!

With inventory accuracy running 18 percent, one "old-timer" was able to find a certain spice in the warehouse by smell (this is a true story)! In an increasingly volatile, increasingly competitive food market, Tone's couldn't afford to keep sniffing around its warehouses with fingers crossed.

The business problems, then, were forecast inaccuracies, the high inventory and inaccuracies in records—quality problems, for sure! One possible solution was to streamline the manufacturing process so customer orders could be produced virtually as they came in, that is, made to order.

The goal was small quantities (lot sizes)—grind and package only what was needed for that day. They also wanted to do away with inspections, storage areas, excessive movement of product, long manufacturing lead times and the various production bottlenecks that had troubled them.

Let's use the tools associated with quality programs to try and get the kind of performance we want. What is our definition of an Ideal Manufacturing Process? Raw materials come into the plant in the morning, finished goods go out in the afternoon, producing no more than the customer needs for that day. That, then, is the expectation. Now let's look at the obstacles to that expectation.

In the case of our spice company, the expectations were:

1) Short manufacturing lead times
2) Reliable availability of material
3) Small order quantities
4) Make only what's needed
5) A balanced flow

The next step was to list the obstacles to meeting those expectations.

1) Poor quality of schedules, both supplier and manufacturing
2) Lack of packaging materials on hand
3) Unstable, unreliable manufacturing and supplier schedules
4) Long changeover times
5) Poor visibility of future capacity requirements
6) Lack of flexibility in the work force
7) Responsibility by inspectors for quality, not at the source

8) Performance measurements that encouraged overproducing

When we put a total quality program in place, we use a series of problem-solving tools such as brainstorming, pareto diagrams, histograms, process control charts, cause and effect diagrams ("fishbone" charts), scatter diagrams and the like. We use these tools—starting with the quality problem—to work backward until we find the real, or root, cause or causes of the problem, which we can attack. Normally, application of these techniques is thought of only in terms of product quality—parts that are too long or material that is too sticky, for example.

But those same problem-solving tools can apply to the other nonconformance issues. In order to overcome the obstacles facing them, Tone's needed what? A valid master schedule, valid capacity plans, high inventory record accuracy, suppliers who could quickly respond to the company's needs, the ability to perform to zero defects (a term coined by Phil Crosby), quick changeovers and a cross-trained work force for flexibility. They also needed the support of everyone in the company to carry off the program.

Following a step-by-step procedure, they attacked those obstacles. Sales worked with Planning on future predictions to establish valid, stable master schedules. The bills of material and the inventory records needed to be better than 18 percent.

Tone's needed to work with their union, the Teamsters, on work rules and job classifications to get cross-training programs off the ground. Traditional performance measurements had to be replaced to allow the workers to take the time to learn new jobs without penalizing the plant manager's score card—in essence, learning to be comfortable running the business differently.

Tone's knew it had to drastically cut changeover times. Changeover times could take three days or longer. They applied the problem-solving techniques to changeovers. Why were they long? Answers ranged from, "Because nobody's ever thought they needed to be shorter," to "equipment design limitations." Each

> **But those same problem-solving tools can apply to the other nonconformance issues.**

45

obstacle was analyzed and broken down, and a series of steps was suggested to overcome each obstacle. Initially, the average changeover time was a few hours. After reducing the average time to less than 20 minutes, Tone's still wasn't satisfied and was convinced more reductions were possible.

Just as important, Tone's realized that for the overall program to work, everyone had to be involved— people involvement is always a key issue. To show that they were serious, Tone's offered everyone in the company a day off with pay if changeovers could be cut in half. Workers were taught the way the production line worked, why machines worked as they did (in fact, a testing program for new workers was established). Old equipment was modified, some of the most significant modifications coming from the line workers themselves. Flexibility, constantly switching to make only what customers ordered, increased as changeover times dropped. The average changeover time is now less than 10 minutes, and Tone's is going for five, working with machine manufacturers to explain why five-minute changeovers are important ("The first time we went to a machine trade show and started talking about five-minute changeovers," a Tone's employee reports, "they looked at us like we'd lost our minds").

> **Tone's offered everyone in the company a day off with pay if changeovers could be cut in half.**

The same logic was applied to inventory record accuracy. Instead of 18 percent inventory accuracy and warehouses navigated by smell, Tone's now sports 98-plus percent accuracy on a substantially reduced inventory. Sometimes there's a synergy that happens: Once inventory accuracy was up and the warehouse was organized, the head of one packaging line noticed that 20 percent of the products, still scattered all over the warehouse, accounted for 80 percent of that line's mix. Those products were moved to a point-of-use storage spot, and productivity took another jump.

The results are impressive. Finished goods inventory spins at 32 times per year, up from 8 turns. Customer service improved from 87 percent on time to more than 99 percent on time.

Profits soared to all-time records! And all of this while the business grew 60 percent in three years.

Understanding Quality with a capital "Q," listening to internal customer expectations and applying the same basic problem-solving tools to all Quality problems were the keys to Tone's success.

Tone's attacked each of the obstacles as quality problems. Notice the continuous improvement—if we can get changeovers down to 10 minutes, why not nine, eight, five, three minutes?

We need to see quality efforts as more than reducing warranty claims. There are many companies whose customers don't perceive them as having a quality problem. Others don't perceive themselves as having a quality problem because they have a large market share. The larger payback from quality improvement efforts—once correctly understood and applied—is usually cost reductions, not warranty reductions. Once a company gets the process of planning, maintaining accurate records, internal suppliers performing to internal customer's expectations—i.e., high quality—the job can be done with less effort, and the savings drop directly to the bottom line and accumulate as higher profits.

The larger payback from quality improvement efforts. . . is usually cost reductions

Once we understand that issues like inventory record accuracy, scheduling, setup time and the like are quality issues, we can simply extend the quality program into areas other than the functionality of the product. The troops see stability, clear direction, a steady course, not the constant implementation of new fads every week. There is one program, the Quality Program. And it's more than a "program." It's a process, an on-going journey. Quality becomes a single commitment and extends into all areas of the company, and a World Class company understands that the quality commitment never ends.

The trick is to see quality with a big "Q," and then apply the problem-solving techniques associated with quality programs across the board. For our spice company, the long changeover times were a quality problem, and were approached as such. So were excess inventory and record accuracy problems.

Another classic quality success story is Eastman Kodak's Copy Products Division. Copy Products makes

47

high end office copiers—definitely treading on Japanese turf! Copy Products had gone the traditional path of trying to inspect quality in—at one point with 100 percent inspection and 350 inspectors on staff.

"In 1983," says Dale Esse, former manager of Quality Assurance, "we recognized many drawbacks in the 100 percent inspection system."

Those drawbacks included:

-One hundred percent inspection is not 100 percent effective.

-One hundred percent inspection is essentially a sorting process of good product from bad.

-One hundred percent inspection is not cost-effective.

"In addition," Kodak officers wrote at the time, "Assembly had little responsibility for quality and no apparent incentive for building it right the first time. QC Inspection acted as a 'police force,' enforcing corrective action after the product was assembled. The accepted philosophy to improve quality was to increase the frequency of inspection."

What changed that philosophy was a tidal wave of high-quality, low-cost competing products from Japan. Copy Products needed higher quality and lower cost.

The plan was to put responsibility for quality back on the source—Assembly—giving them the training and empowering them to make quality changes.

When Copy Products began their program, they had an average of 30 major defects per machine. They had one inspector for every three people making copiers. Twenty-five percent of the cost of assembling each machine went toward paying an inspector's salary, and 12 percent of each month's operating budget went to pay for parts that had to be scrapped.

After three years, quality improved so dramatically, they began measuring major defects per 1000 machines.

Kodak reported:

-Overall reduction in nonconformity per unit of 90 percent.

-A 70 percent reduction of QA personnel with a direct labor savings of $3 million since 1985.

-A 50 percent reduction in QA unit cost.

-Significant reduction of rework cost—from 12.5 percent to .8 percent in one product line alone.

Copy Products took a number of innovative steps in addition to putting the responsibility for quality back at the source.

They set up quality circles so the people who built the machines could tell management how to better assemble them. They opened the company's books to the employees. They put up charts and graphs measuring productivity, quality, costs, delivery schedules and the like. For the first time, hourly employees had a say in how each department was run. Kodak began working with suppliers to assure quality components.

And, when a department or a team or a person did well, everyone celebrated.

Kodak Copy Products now has 25 inspectors.

"If you walk around the place, talk to both white and blue collar workers," says the television documentary, *The Quality Revolution,* "you get the feeling that having QC inspectors was never a good idea."

"You kept making the same mistakes over and over again," says Frances Harris, who works at Copy Products, "because you knew if something was wrong, they would just call you and you would fix it."

"It sounds kind of silly," says veteran Copy Products employee Marlaine Zaffuto. "I was one who never believed we needed QC in the first place. When I build a copier, I build it like I'm taking it home...I don't want to go over my work twice. I try to do it right the first time."

A quality researcher visited a Toyota plant in Japan and asked the plant manager how many quality inspectors were employed there.

"Three thousand," the manager replied, the total number of people employed at the plant.

Although quality from a warranty angle may not improve, (although we've found that not to be the case), direct labor costs, overhead and general administration expenses are drastically cut as quality improves.

For the first time, hourly employees had a say in how each department was run.

49

There's less changeover time, no "extras" left over, less inventory, easier maintenance of records, easier implementation of engineering changes, even fewer data transactions, which may mean that we don't have to upgrade the computer system this year. Capacity is increased without more capital when equipment is used to make only the right items without rework. Setup time becomes run time. There are intangible benefits on the shop floor as well. The push for flexible capacity means that workers have more variety in their jobs, plus more of a sense of being part of the company—an advantage that can't be underestimated! The greater the people involvement, the more chance we have of staying ahead in the Competitive Race.

There are two other critical points about quality. The first is to be patient—the gains aren't going to be showing up next quarter. The second comes from Dr. Deming, who points out that everyone's best efforts alone will not accomplish the goal of higher quality.

"Best efforts," he wrote, "to be effective, require guidance to move in the right direction. It is especially important that top managers know what their job is."

DISCUSSION POINTS

1) Have your quality improvement efforts focused primarily on product and components?

2) Based on the idea that quality is conformance to expectations, list 10 examples of nonconformance with internal customers.

3) Estimate the cost of nonconformances for the 10 examples discussed in Question 2.

4) Determine who is responsible for the nonconformances identified in Question 2.

5) Are nonconformances occurring because people are unwilling to conform or because the expectations aren't clear?

6) Define a "defect." Discuss the principles of variability and how they apply to the problems identified in Question 2.

7) What appear to be the root causes of the problems identified in Question 2?

8) Discuss how acceptable "tolerances" are established. Discuss the impact of tolerances on costs.

9) Discuss the difference between tolerances and statistically calculated limits.

10) How well do your people understand basic problem-solving, facilitating and team-building techniques? What efforts are under way to enhance these skills?

CHAPTER 4

Maximizing the Human Asset Account

Every morning when Johnny Jones shows up for work at Feel Good's Southport plant, he picks up his time card and turns off his brain.

At least, that's what they think I do, Johnny thinks one grim Monday morning. Monday was particularly grim because Johnny and the other 20 people on the welding line had put in a full eight hours on Saturday trying to humor a couple of engineers who wanted to know why the line kept backing up. The Engineering guys figured they could re-engineer the pc board stuffer for "around a quarter-mil," and that should take care of the bogged-down line.

Johnny hadn't said a thing, mostly because the two suits looked through him, like he was some kind of bug. Or maybe invisible. Quarter of a million dollars to fix the machine, which was a laugh, because it wasn't the machine that wasn't working right. It was a whole bunch of little stuff, like the guys were talking about in the bar after work. Silly having the parts warehouse on the other side of the plant, always running out of parts and having to send someone back and forth. Tools scattered all over the place, except where you needed them. Plus, sign the tools out, then sign them back in. He'd talked to a couple of people upstairs about that one, like they were going to run off with the socket wrenches or something. The people upstairs just shrugged; they knew it was stupid, but, hey, that's the way it was.

True, Johnny thought, the machine was a bear to adjust, but mostly because the machine's designers had never figured it'd be used the way Feel Good was using it. One day Johnny had taken his supervisor out

---

PEOPLE

OLD PARADIGM

- Need Supervision
- Workers Work, Managers Think
- Can't be Trusted
- Adversarial Relationship, worker to Manager
- Manage People

NEW PARADIGM

- Self-Managed
- Everyone is a Problemsolver
- Trust
- Teamwork
- Lead People

for a drink and shown him some plans he'd drawn up to make the machine much easier to adjust, cost a couple of hundred max, and Johnny'd come in and do the welding on Sunday.

"And when did you get your engineering degree?" his supervisor had wanted to know. "Do you know how much these machines cost?"

Johnny had shrugged it off, but it galled, you know. He'd built his kid's racing go-kart from the ground up, and he figured his kid's safety was worth more than the machine. But, hey, if Feel Good wanted to spend a quarter-mil on the machine, more power to 'em. He had a bumper sticker on his car that summed it up: "Happiness is seeing Feel Good Inc. in the rearview mirror."

Heck, he just worked there.

In the long run, there have probably been no more damaging words to American industry than, "I just work here."

We are willing to spend millions of dollars on new equipment, hardware, software, yet we blanch when it comes to spending money on people. People—which we say are our most important resource—don't show up on our balance sheet at all. A potential buyer for our company might look at our P&Ls, our capital investments, our patents, and never look at our *people* investment.

"Most American companies still view workers as a cost that should be minimized," MIT's Dr. Michael Dertouzos told the *Wall Street Journal* recently, "not as a resource to be developed."

Harvard's Richard E. Walton, a top theorist on employee involvement, puts it even more bluntly: "To have World Class quality and costs and the ability to assimilate new technology," he says, "we must have the world's best ability to develop human capabilities."

In the old paradigm, workers didn't have brains. Workers, as Frederick W. Taylor so well articulated, did what they were told. We developed a paternal "chain-of-command" to "manage" the workers, tell them what to do. We justified the chain-of-command by saying there was a problem with the "work ethic"—people wouldn't work unless they were forced to work by overseers. Workers couldn't be trusted—got to watch them all the time. That's why the shop floor punched a clock and management didn't.

And workers responded accordingly. "Work," one shop floor operator told us, "is nothing but an eight-hour interruption of my leisure time." Over the years, workers and management developed an adversarial relationship.

One of the most telling comments we've ever heard was from a CEO who was having the proverbial million $20-problems. We asked if he'd sat down and talked to some of the people on the shop floor about these problems. He smiled and pointed at a cartoon framed on his wall. It showed a picture of a pig obviously attempting to sing.

"Never try to teach a pig to sing," the caption read. "It wastes your time and annoys the pig."

No danger of a mixed message there, is there?

That "singing pig" message had managed to percolate throughout the entire company. The guys in suits think, the guys without suits work.

What do you think the likelihood of our CEO getting any problem-solving help from the "singing pigs" is?

"For a long time we thought of the hourly employees as coming to work with hands and forgetting they had a brain," Lockheed-California Co. director of productivity R.P. Leifer told *Business Week*.

Of all the paradigms listed in this book, the idea of "checking your brain at the door when you pick up your time card" is probably the most pervasive in American industry. Yet, ironically, it is also the single biggest factor in achieving the goals of World Class performance. That's because of the changing nature of the problem. We've already gone through our meat-axe period of slashing bodies from the payroll; we've closed factories and laid off whole towns. We've streamlined and merged and juggled all over the place, and we still have problems. As we've said earlier, they're small problems, $20 problems. These little problems resist

Work. . .is nothing but an 8-hour interruption of my leisure time.

55

having money thrown at them and are virtually immune to Engineering SWAT teams and Vice Presidents In Charge Of Little Problems. Sometimes it's hard—no, impossible—for the guys in suits to even recognize these problems. It takes the people who are closest to the problems to identify the $20 problems and begin creating solutions.

Our people have the skills as well. They've managed their own lives, handled personal, club, church and business finances, raised families, renovated houses, tinkered with cars—in fact, routinely done all of what we refer to as "management" functions. They understand problem-solving, because it's a part of people's everyday life. It's only through an enormous and false conceit that we came to believe that people had to be told every little thing to do.

A company we consulted with had a setup time problem. Tools were centralized, and whenever a machine operator needed to do a setup or a machine alignment, which was often, the operator checked a wrench out of the storeroom, made the adjustment and returned the wrench to the storeroom.

Management wanted to focus on automation, robots, rearranging the factory. Why not, we suggested, give all the machine operators their own wrenches, as one of the floor people had suggested to us? Problem solved, and for less than $100.

Of course, they're not all that easy, but our wrench story points out what the real problem is in solving all those detail problems.

Would the CEO of the company have been able to make a decision to purchase the wrenches? He or she might have the authority, certainly, but suppose we're talking about a Fortune 500 manufacturing company with plants around the country. The CEO can't possibly be aware of every machine operator's special problems. Most general managers, plant managers and shift supervisors aren't tuned into this level of detail. And they shouldn't be.

The people involvement conundrum is not just tied to the shop floor, either. Throughout the company there are people with good ideas—ideas they're not telling us. Take the Sales Department, for example. We say we can't forecast accurately what products we'll be selling. Our salesmen, though, are very probably on some kind of commission schedule. Their livelihood depends on knowing what they're going to sell, and you can bet they have a very good idea of how many of which products are going to sell. Yet that critical input never seems to find its way into the forecast.

There are other examples throughout the company. The typing pool has great ideas about reducing paperwork, because paper is all they handle. The people in Purchasing probably have excellent ideas about working better with our suppliers. On the shop floor, as in our example, some of our most persistent engineering problems already have solutions crafted by our line workers.

But no one is asking, or listening.

So, too many times, the million $20-problems have been ignored, unsolved.

But the increasing globalization of the market means there are more and more companies in the game, which means more and more *good* companies are out there competing. For us to continue to compete, we've got to gnaw away at those small problems, and the only way we're going to accomplish that is to empower our people and turn them loose.

We get an interesting batch of mixed comments when we say this in class. Someone invariably cites the old saw, which goes, "Who says work is supposed to be fun? We're running a factory, not a country club."

In 1987, Volvo decided to create an automobile factory without assembly lines to assemble the Volvo 740 sedan. Instead of the traditional assembly line carry-over from Henry Ford's day, a group of seven to 10 work teams assembles the entire car.

"We're not doing this because we're nice guys," Volvo president Roger Holtback told *Business Week*. "We're not doing this because we like experiments."

Volvo did it for the bottom line—the experimental plant produced cars in fewer hours and of better quality than the company's three other Swedish plants.

Think about that: The bottom line.

Throughout the company, there are people with good ideas. . . but no one is asking—or listening.

"All our people programs are based on the bottom line," says Trane's Bruce Achenbach. "The intent of people programs is not to enhance the workplace, although that is a welcome and important side effect. It's about money."

We can't be World Class without our people working with us.

Period.

In our classes, approximately half thinks the idea of trusting our people to solve our problems is like "Mom and apple pie," a given. The other half thinks we've lost our minds—"Who could trust those guys?"

Obviously, the schism between management and labor runs deep. American manufacturing grew up in the early, unenlightened days of the Industrial Revolution, where people really did seem to be cogs in a huge machine. This was further heightened by scientific management engineers such as Frederick Taylor, who sought to make direct labor more efficient.

Over the years, the tension has been heightened by such diverse factors as the adversarial relationship between unions and management and the acceptance of many layers of "management" as necessary. In fact, Joe Cox, former CEO at Centrilift, an oil pump manufacturer, told us the whole language of "management" was onerous.

"You manage *things*," he said. "You *lead* people."

I recently participated, along with Tom Peters and others, in a television special titled *The Quality Revolution*, and one thing in particular struck me. An autoworker was galled by the phrase "make it idiot-proof," because, to him, it was very clear who management thought the idiots were.

Both sides contributed to the alienation process. Management was insensitive to the workers' needs, knowledge and abilities; workers, for their part, were often unwilling to accept the changes and new ideas at face value.

We can't be World Class without our people working with us.

The Problem With Involvement

The problem with involvement is a simple one: The topic is huge.

When we talk about employee involvement, what do we mean? A suggestion box next to the time clock or autonomous work groups that set their own hours, do their own hiring and firing? Do we mean informally asking around the office or at the coffee pot before we start a new project, or do we mean a formal system that seeks to empower employees at every level of the decision-making process?

Employee involvement is a complicated process. It is not simply a suggestion box, although a suggestion box may well be part of the involvement process. It's not a coffee urn roundtable, a bull session, even a series of meetings.

Employee involvement can be looked at as a continuum that runs from a reports meeting—the familiar meeting where everyone reads his or her report—through project teams, roundtables, action teams—all the way to autonomous work teams. We can also break employee involvement down into three basic levels: problem-solving teams, special-purpose teams and self-managing teams.

Problem-solving teams are similar to Japanese quality circles, an idea that reached its peak in the late 1970s (although the idea had been around American industry since the 1920s). Problem-solving teams are just that, teams organized to discuss ways of solving specific problems, such as quality problems. Discussion, though, is usually where a problem-solving team stops. The resulting ideas are passed up the organizational chart for action.

Special-purpose teams, sort of internal SWAT teams, are the next step up from the problem-solving teams. They have the power to implement changes and may cut across divisional lines.

Self-managing teams, or autonomous work groups, are the ultimate results, teams that produce products and handle many of what were traditional managerial jobs themselves.

For employee involvement to work, there's got to be a baseline change in our attitudes, a shift in the paradigm. "I think; you work" just won't work.

The new paradigm calls for involvement at all levels. We want everyone chipping away at the small problems that hobble our efficiency. For that paradigm to work, our employees need to know why we want to make the changes, and how the changes can be made.

If people involvement is such a good idea, why isn't every company doing something about it? There are six main obstacles to achieving the new paradigm, coming both from management and workers.

1) A reward system that motivates people not to get involved.

2) A lack of understanding of the root problems.

3) A threat to the existing supervisory base.

4) A lack of action on suggestions or ideas.

5) The threat of losing your job as a result of increased productivity.

6) Management misunderstanding of the bottom line benefits of people involvement.

The Wrong Reward

Take the case of our salesperson. He or she knows he can sell 1,000 units a month. There haven't been any sophisticated marketing surveys, focus groups or necessarily a lot of time hunched over the old computer. But what he or she has is a finger on the marketplace. Call it instinct, call it gut reaction, good salespeople either ride the market or quickly become unemployed.

This salesperson also knows that there's a bonus for *exceeding* quota. If the salesperson is comfortable with the 1,000 widgets number, is he or she going to put down that number as quota? Probably not. Instead, projected sales might be listed as 850 units, with a 150 "fudge factor." All throughout the company there are fudge factors here and fudge factors there, until everyone breaks out laughing when they read the numbers. Which leads to a high degree of variation in demand, with the accompanying big swings in the schedule.

> **The new paradigm calls for involvement at all levels.**

There are other signals we send. On the shop floor, for example, we might pay an operator by the piece, rewarding the operator for producing to the max and sorting through the piles to find "easy ones," not necessarily what the customer ordered. Or middle management might be focusing on increasing machine utilization or minimizing the direct labor variance. The machine operator might know that we may not need a couple of thousand extra widget subassemblies, but why should he tell us?

Many times, either management or workers might not understand the root causes of problems. Many times, the root causes aren't that obvious. All through this book we'll be looking at the hidden causes behind productivity problems.

We want to move away from the old paradigm of a strict hierarchical job structure to a flatter organizational chart. Each layer of management is an impediment to communications. It's like the old demonstration of misinformation we all learned in grade school. The teacher tells one class a bit of information, then instructs the students to pass it on. After a few days, the piece of information has gone through so many retellings that it is unrecognizable. We want to encourage teamwork and worker input—in fact, we want all our workers to be thinking, to be helping on those million $20-problems. Every level of management the necessary information must go through decreases the chance that the information is going to get all the way upstream, and that the responsive action is going to get downstream.

Second, let's apply our concepts of continuous improvement to levels of management. Bruce Achenbach points out that many of the management levels not only don't add value, but were put in place to more efficiently "manage" the workers.

"We've put into place rules and levels of management to 'catch' the bad apples," he says, "and it doesn't work. There's a small percentage of people who are going to be problems, and there's nothing you can do about that. Why should we spend hundreds of thousands of dollars and inconvenience everybody else

Each layer of management is an impediment to communications.

trying to catch them."

As a quick example of Achenbach's thesis, what about the whole management level that does nothing but keep track of workers' time? Johnny Jones got stuck on the Interstate and was two minutes late punching in today, so we need to dock him 10 minutes' pay. We've invested in a time clock system, a whole sub-department in Accounting to compile the time on a daily basis, new report software so we'll have the total lost minutes at our fingertips, real time, on-line, new software for Finance that allows us to refigure everybody's wages on a weekly basis and a whole host of other non-value adding activities. What we've succeeded in doing with all this paperwork, hardware and activity is turning Johnny Jones into our enemy—he only works here, remember.

At companies like Trane and Centrilift, the move has been toward autonomous work groups. Like Volvo's assembly teams, work groups are essentially teams that produce an entire product. Depending on the company, the teams may have the power to set their times, responsibilities, shifts, schedules, even vacation time and overtime. At Trane, work groups have veto power in hiring group members. Both Trane and Centrilift have done away with time clocks and the associated non-value adding baggage. Instead, the work groups handle all employee scheduling.

Guess what has happened to tardiness and absenteeism?

It hasn't disappeared, of course, but it has decreased. The work groups take pride in their product and their group. Instead of time clocks and the "company police," people show up on time because they have a responsibility to their fellow workers.

At Centrilift, for the autonomous work groups, days absent dropped from 76 days a year to 34 days a year in a two-year period. Productivity increased by 34 percent, scrap was reduced by 56 percent and no time was lost to accidents. Again, pride worked better—much better—than rules and regulations.

We've got other major obstacles to the new paradigm.

There's often resistance from supervisors and middle management. How would you feel when the new hotshot comes in and starts talking about trimming the management tree, and you're one of the branches she wants to cut off? The same for supervisors, who often came up through the shop floor over years or decades. The solution to this one is tricky, because, honestly, not everyone is going to make the cut. But the most successful World Class companies have been equally successful in moving or retraining supervisors and middle management for other positions.

This ties in with point number five, no lost jobs for increased productivity. We ask our people for labor-saving ideas, get one that allows the work to be done by four people instead of five, then send the fifth one home because our productivity has increased and we don't need as many workers. When we ask our people for those "labor-saving" ideas again, what do you think is going to happen?

What would *you* do?

Instead of laying people off, we want to retrain—cross-train—them, to create a flexible work force. Cross-trained workers provide a lot of pluses for a company. We can move labor to where we need it, adding to our flexibility in responding to the market. The workers like it, because it adds variety to the job. Cross-training is also a valid response to two increasing problems for industry—the continued shortage of skilled workers and the rapidly changing skills necessary for modern workers.

"Today's technology has telescoped product and process life cycles so much," says John Stepp, U.S. deputy undersecretary of labor, "that skills are becoming obsolete at a breathtaking pace. Instead of paying for a job, employers are now paying for a variety of skills that workers acquire."

"We used to hire people because they could manipulate parts, they could put things together with their hands," Motorola's director of planning, Susan Hooker, told *Fortune* magazine. "Now we really need the whole worker. You have to have somebody to do simple programming, read, write commands, interpret information on terminals and do preventive maintenance."

After deciding to create a compensation system that rewarded people for learning new skills, Motorola's defect rate on cellular phones fell 77 percent, from 1,000 defects per million parts to 223.

With cross-training, we also bring a new pair of eyes to solving our million $20-problems, which has proven to be a major plus at numerous companies. Think back to our theory of paradigms. The people who are the most "locked into" the old paradigms are the people who have the most invested in them. Outsiders are more likely to see new solutions, new paradigms, because they're not fully "vested" in the old system. There's also a noticeable increase in quality as workers learn more about the process. At Tone's in Des Moines, for example, a number of quality problems were "headed off at the pass" when newly cross-trained workers caught problems on the line that had previously gone unnoticed.

There are obstacles to a flexible work force, though.

Look at job classifications, for instance. Job classifications grew out of labor's fear of being abused by management and as a way of preserving the hierarchical seniority system. But in the new paradigm, in a World Class performance environment, we want our workers to be as flexible as possible. All the companies mentioned in this book have some kind of cross-training programs either on-line or in the works. But rigid job classifications are an impediment.

At many World Class companies, the number of job classifications is shrinking dramatically. National Steel, for example, struck a deal with the United Steelworkers Union that allowed them to consolidate 78 job titles into 16. The result? National can now produce a ton of steel in 4.3 man-hours versus 5.5 in 1984.

Dozens of job classifications can usually be lumped under a single category. At Trane, for example, that category is "Production Technician," and employees are rewarded for increasing their skills in

With cross-training, we also bring a new pair of eyes to solving our million $20-problems.

other areas. Originally, skills acquisition was tied to the work groups—if their production team was making their numbers, the individual is rewarded. But the workers were uncomfortable with that system, and Trane, in keeping with their people philosophy, changed their pay-for-skills plan accordingly.

A second obstacle, as mentioned earlier, is the issue of supervisors. As our workers take more and more of the responsibility for their own supervision, the classic "supervisor"—the person who walked around the shop floor and made sure everybody was busy, is withering away. Supervisors got caught in a paradigm "swirl." Instead of cracking the whip or functioning as expediter, supervisors are now being asked to help communicate, to facilitate new ideas and to help with teamwork. We owe those supervisors the additional training to fit into the new paradigm.

For example, at Intermec Corp., manufacturers of data collection equipment, they're experimenting with what they call the dual career path, which basically allows an engineer good at being creative but not interested in administrative duties, to rise in the company. Others, more interested and skilled in leading and motivating people, can rise through the traditional path. In the old paradigm, it was strictly move up or move out, and the way to move up was into supervision, which caused the company to lose the talents of many individuals. Trane has had a similar dual career path for 10 years.

The Boogie Woogie Flu?

It's easy to see the symptoms. Products that don't work. Warehouses overflowing with inventory. Work-in-process piled all over the shop floor. New products that creep toward the market at a snail's pace.

It's a lot harder, though, to see the actual disease. In fact, it may be impossible to see the disease—the paradigm we use to run our business—unless we take some basic steps.

First, we've got to educate our people. Everyone, from the executive suite to the receptionist's desk,

Supervisors are now being asked to help communicate, to facilitate and to help.

needs to understand why achieving World Class performance standards is important and what strategy we'll be using to achieve that performance. We were impressed recently while talking to several people from Compaq Computer. Everyone we talked to had a surprisingly good grasp of not only the company's goals, but the huge stakes that were involved.

We need to make sure that our people see the relationship between winning the competitive race and their own standard of living. Partly as a throwback to the 1960s, where the entire concept of *competition* came under fire, we tend to not have the gut-level connection between winning and our job security. Because of the explosive growth of the American economy in the 1950s and 1960s, the idea of *competing to win* was lost in the shuffle of growth. Most of the companies mentioned in this book have taken steps to introduce the people who work in the company to their competition. It can be as simple as a competing company's ad thumbtacked to a bulletin board. The important thing, though, is to create a sense of urgency that there is, in fact, a race going on, and that there will be winners—and losers.

> **Everyone needs to understand why achieving world class performance standards is important.**

Obviously, to get that level of understanding, we're talking about more than a couple of hours in a classroom. Once again, instead of *education*, we're talking about a paradigm shift, a change in the way we do business. Here's another quick analogy about the difference—probably every adult in the United States knows that the way to lose weight is through a sensible diet and moderate exercise. So since we are *educated* about diet, no one has any trouble losing weight, right? That's the difference between acquiring knowledge and behavioral change.

Before we can effect that change, our people have to:

1) Understand the reasons for the change and what they stand to gain.

2) Have the knowledge to understand the causes of the disease rather than just the symptoms.

3) Have the communication and problem-solving skills necessary to carry out changes.

If all three of those items aren't in place, any people-involvement effort is doomed.

Leadership—not management—is critical for any employee involvement program to work. Leaders need to be able to focus on the problems, directing, guiding, facilitating, listening and responding in a timely manner.

One of the most interesting employee involvement efforts in the country is happening in Macon, Georgia, at the Trane Company. One of 13 plants nationwide, Trane builds huge commercial air conditioners. The Macon plant is relatively new, and General Manager Bruce Achenbach knew from the beginning that he wanted maximum employee involvement.

In fact, what he wanted was for employees to run the plant. But before they could get to that point, Achenbach's management team realized that communications skills were critical.

"We were going to be asking our people to communicate with us," he says. "That assumes that they—and we—know how to communicate."

To overcome the barriers to communication, and to facilitate the level of people involvement Trane hoped for, all Trane employees went through 40 hours of communications and problem-solving techniques.

"All of a sudden, we had communications all over the place," says Achenbach. "Then we realized that there was another necessary step."

In addition to the communications' training, Trane added an additional 10 hours in *team-building*. That way, everybody understands the tools and techniques available for problem-solving, as well as the dynamics of working in teams, before they begin chipping away at the million $20-problems.

Trane also has a unique program for increasing communication. It's called the Name Game, and it's played on company time in the cafeteria. Basically, it's a pretty simple game: The moderator reads off facts about a Trane employee, and everyone gets to guess who that employee is. The questions might be relatively painless—who has a strange middle name—to who has what hobby to mildly ribald joking. No one is exempt from the ribbing, from the CEO on down to the people in the mailroom. The result is that, in addition to some good laughs, the employees of Trane, from the top to the bottom, feel themselves to be part of a team. Because Trane's relatively small management team (nine managers for 135 employees) always participates, the Name Game has proven more effective than an "Open Door Policy" in making management accessible.

"We were kind of worried when we started the Name Game," Achenbach says. "But now people really love it."

The new paradigm sounds almost too "New Age" to be true. Trust your people; give them the tools and they'll come through for you.

Isn't it worth a try?

DISCUSSION POINTS

1) Do you have on-going training in group problem-solving techniques, facilitation and communication skills?

2) Do you encourage, recognize and act upon suggestions? Do you measure the volume of suggestions per employee?

3) Do you have an active program to reduce supervision and flatten the organizational chart?

4) Do you have a plan to retrain and reassign excess supervisory people? Are they comfortable with the plan?

5) Have you taken a survey or unbiased reading to ensure everyone is comfortable making recommendations for changes, even if those suggestions are critical of current policies? Does everyone in the company believe their job is thinking, not just working?

6) Have you clearly and forcefully communicated that no one will be laid off if new ideas improve productivity and the result is excess people?

7) Are compensation systems a help or a hindrance to participative decision-making?

8) Is time set aside most days for production people to do something productive other than make product?

9) Have the number of job classifications on the plant floor been reduced to one or two? If not, why not?

10) Does everyone thoroughly understand and accept that more participatory, self-managed work groups are essential to cost reduction?

The Importance Of Speed

"**W**hen a new paradigm appears," wrote Joel Arthur Barker in *Discovering The Future*, "everyone goes back to zero."

Which means, simply, that when a paradigm changes, all the leverage you might have had in the old paradigm disappears. When the Japanese sprung quality on an unsuspecting world, for example, even the most successful businesses shook.

Why?

Because the rules themselves had changed. Companies that had prided themselves on 98 percent yield—that is, a two percent scrap factor—suddenly found themselves facing a world where the new unit of measure was *defects per million parts*.

Everybody went back to zero.

Except, of course, the paradigm shifters. They found themselves in the enviable position of having named the new game, and they set the new rules. For the brief period of time the rest of the world plays catch-up, the paradigm shifters own the market.

One of the lessons we should have learned from the quality revolution of the 1970s and 1980s is that the quality revolution is neither the last nor the only revolution in manufacturing we're going to have to face.

The quality revolution, to a large part, has been successful. In a recent survey we commissioned, we found that product quality was the overwhelming priority for American business executives. Quality *is* up.

But what happens when everybody's door closes? When all the clocks keep the right time? Already, in Japan, quality is the *ante*. You can't even get to the starting line for the competitive race without superb product quality. We're already starting to see a similar trend in the best American companies—quality is becoming a given.

So where is the competitive edge for the 1990s and beyond?

Flexibility.

Flexibility, or as Trane puts it more simply, *speed*, is rapidly becoming the cutting edge for World Class companies.

"If the '80s were the decade of quality," Bruce J. Haupt, former director of Advanced Manufacturing Systems for IBM, told *Modern Materials Handling* magazine, "the '90s will be the decade of time—as reflected in customer responsiveness, rapid market entry and product quality."

Haupt's comments are backed up by our own survey of 4,000 manufacturing executives. While product quality was the clear winner in priorities, on-time delivery, cost reductions and new product introductions were close behind. On-time deliveries and new product introductions fall under the broad heading of flexibility.

Simply put, flexibility is a company's ability to respond to the market. The Association of Manufacturing Excellence refers to flexibility as "a short lead-time-to-change," noting that almost everything— product design, customer order specifications, output volume, product mix and technology, to name just a few—can change. More specifically, we define flexibility as excellence in three areas:

1) Rapid response to shifts in product mix and volume increases or decreases

2) Quickly customizing products for specific customers

3) Shortening the time to bring new products to market

Why the focus on flexibility? Why not cost reduction or some other area of manufacturing? Remember that we're moving to a customer-driven market. A successful music producer, when asked how he had been able to sell millions and millions of records in pop music and jazz and country, has a simple answer.

Flexibility is a company's ability to respond to the market.

"The friends and neighbors always speak," he said. "And the friends and neighbors are always right." Music is a purely customer-driven market—people buy records they like. The gauge of the success of a music producer is how well that producer meets the expectations of his customers—sales, in other words.

As all markets become more and more customer-driven, an interesting thing happens with the customers. Like the burger chain's jingle chants, they want it their way. They want it red, or with tail fins, or with a remote control. Customers become accustomed to variety; they *expect* variety, whether that variety is color, new packaging, or technological innovation. The companies that meet those customer expectations are the companies that are going to win the competitive race.

Second, as the competitive race has moved onto a global track, there are more companies in the race. That means there are more *good* companies in the race. There are more companies who are willing to fill those niches—tail fins, red paint, remote controls—than there used to be. If you're not willing to meet your customers' expectations, your competition will be.

As the competitive race has moved onto a global track, there are more companies in the race.

The old paradigms for American manufacturing are relentlessly inflexible. In fact, the whole concept of "mass production" is built around producing large numbers of the same item for an economy of scale. The less change, the better. Remember Henry Ford's classic comment on the first Fords? "You can have them in any color you want, as long as it's black."

In today's market, the line is more like, "You can have them in any color you want. Period." And, oh yes, the customer would like it later this afternoon.

How do we accomplish this apparent miracle and meet our customers' expectations?

We are flexible.

How do we become flexible?

That's what the rest of this book is about.

We've looked at the necessity for quality and people involvement—without those two items firmly in place, the path to World Class is ultimately hopeless. The following chapters begin honing our flexibility.

We become flexible by becoming fast. We become fast by examining the way we've traditionally run our businesses.

If we're willing to examine the ways we've chosen to run our businesses, then make the necessary shifts, we can gain that critical edge on our competitors. The first step in gaining that edge is a reality check—how do we do business now? It's also helpful to understand the *whys* of how we do business now, how our manufacturing businesses have grown the way they have.

Let's look at an example we use in class, Aunt Molly's peppermint candy.

Everybody, no doubt, has an Aunt Molly. She makes perfect candy, every time. Our Aunt Molly makes candy for her favorite teller at the bank. She makes the candy in her work cell, which she persists in calling "the kitchen," working from a bill of material, which she calls the recipe. She has one supplier—the supermarket down on the corner.

She goes to the grocery store, buys the sugar, the flavoring and the like, comes home, measures, mixes and blends the ingredients, cooks the candy, packages the candy and gives it away to friends and relatives.

Her nephew, after tasting Aunt Molly's peppermint candy, realizes he has a gold mine on his hands. All Aunt Molly has to do is make 100 boxes of peppermint candy a week, instead of the single box for the bank teller or Cousin Fred.

So she adds a little to the kitchen, talks a couple of nieces into helping her out, and begins manufacturing Aunt Molly's Famous Peppermint Candy. She still buys the ingredients, mixes, blends, cooks and packages, but things are starting to get more complicated. Whereas before, she could do all the figuring in her head, now she's starting to jot calculations on paper towels. The nieces are adding up their needs on pocket calculators, and the supermarket on the corner has taken to stocking extra amounts of sugar.

Her nephew, ever the entrepreneur, discovers that Aunt Molly also has an old family recipe for lemon drops, and pretty soon there are two products.

And a small factory.

The first step is: how do we do business now?

And not just nieces and nephews, but workers as well.

And a marketing director who suggests that Aunt Molly, Inc., needs a complete line of candies, not just peppermints and lemon drops, to stay in the market-place.

And two more factories.

And even more workers.

A distribution network; special label candies for the big chain stores; special packaging for the holidays.

The complexity has increased. More people need to know what their role is at Aunt Molly, Inc. There are more calculations to be made, more detail plans to be drawn up.

And the risk has gone up. When it was just Aunt Molly, the biggest risk was forgetting a nephew at Christmas or not having a few extra dollars. If Aunt Molly, Inc., makes a major mistake, it can mean lost jobs, broken lives, uprootings and repossessions. The stakes are higher.

Aunt Molly still needs to do the same things. She needs to decide what products to make—Master Schedule. She needs to get the raw materials and a multitude of packaging supplies from her suppliers in the amounts she needs to make those products—Purchasing. She still needs to know how much she is going to make and when she is going to make it—Planning. Aunt Molly has to make the product—Manufacturing—and deliver that product to the marketplace—Distribution. And someone—Finance—still has to total up the score.

When she was in her kitchen making one box of peppermint candy, life was a lot easier. Once a week she needed to make one box of peppermint candy. When she needed to know how much sugar she had to make the candy, she simply opened the pantry door and took physical inventory—she looked. She still needs to know how much she needs and how much she has. Maybe she needs a computer. She needs reliable suppliers. Before, all she needed to do was ask Bob the grocer to add a couple of sacks of sugar to her regular order. She needs new candy to compete in the tricky candy marketplace. She needs a way of measuring how well Aunt Molly, Inc., is really doing.

She needs all the above and more, because the *Candy Trade News* just announced that Uncle Harry, Inc., will be entering the market, introducing a full line of candies from their automated factories in Poland. Their flagship candy will be Authentic Peppermint Drops.

Both Aunt Molly and Aunt Molly, Inc., have a planning system. Both have to deal with the same issues. At each stage, Aunt Molly took the steps that seemed the most likely to produce the desired results.

What changed was the size and complexity of the business, and, as the size and complexity changed, so did the solutions to the problems. It's one thing to have an extra five-pound sack of sugar in the pantry; another thing entirely to have $5 million tied up in sugar inventory. It's one thing to make an extra dozen lemon drops to snack on around the house; quite another to run the fully automated lemon drop machine 24-hours-a-day, 7-days-a-week. The consequences are far more extreme.

What also changed was the candy market itself. Aunt Molly, Inc., now needs to be able to respond to a huge, unexpected order from a chain of discount stores while at the same time doing a limited run of bonbons pegged to the summer's biggest hit movie. Aunt Molly was able to decide between making peppermint candy and lemon drops by asking the neighborhood kids what they wanted. Aunt Molly, Inc., needs the flexibility to respond to a far larger, and, at times, a far more capricious market.

We no longer have the luxury of pretending that it's still business as usual at Aunt Molly's.

Not if we want to survive.

In the next few chapters, we'll be looking at the nuts and bolts of the manufacturing business. What we want to do is isolate the old paradigms, see what they are and the trouble they've caused, then see what the new paradigm should look like.

Narrow the focus a little; peer through the zoom lens. As we look closer at speed, we see what that new paradigm looks like:

1) The factory of the future is quick to respond to market shifts and changes in product mix.

2) That response time is facilitated by everyone in the factory working from a single, integrated sales/manufacturing/financial plan.

3) It also requires World Class suppliers, who understand the necessity for speed.

4) The whole concept of bringing new products to market must change to support the fast, flexible factory of the future.

5) Performance measurements must motivate, evaluate what's necessary to evaluate and reward, not discourage.

DISCUSSION POINTS

      1) Discuss three significant new demands in your markets.

      2) Discuss what flexibility or speed means in your company.

      3) What are the main impediments to increasing your flexibility?

      4) Using the Aunt Molly candy analogy, discuss the changing "complexity" of your business.

The Factory Of The Future

What worried the foreman more than anything else was that the noise level had dropped. The bigger metal cutters over in the east wing, which cut metal for the analyzer boxes, were down—their steady *r..i..i..i..p* sound of sheared aluminum strangely absent. The foreman had already made one trip over to the east wing, and the problem was that they were caught up.

"Well, don't just sit there with your thumb in your nose," the foreman told his machine operators. "Make *something*."

Then he got on the horn to scheduling and raised heck, trying to get them to release some orders to get the machine back on line.

"Listen," he'd said, exasperated. "It takes two days to get these big babies set up for a job, so we'd be crazy not to run everything we've got. You know how much trouble it is to set up for different size boxes!"

Besides, thought the foreman grimly, who the heck knew what they'd be needing next week, anyway? Surely not the scheduler. That poor girl was always in a state of nervous breakdown.

About the only person who knew anything was the guy in the red tennis shoes who came running through about 9:30 every morning with the hot list, slapping red tags on this skid or that skid, or wheeling in on a forklift with a whole new skid of material to be run. Lately the foreman noticed he'd showed up with yellow tags, which were "Hot Hot HOT STUFF," stop everything and run it right now or else.

The else was never specified.

The foreman had asked his boss about the crash and burn problems, but he'd just shrugged it off. You

FACTORY OF THE FUTURE

OLD PARADIGM

- Produce Maximum
- Large Lot Sizes
- Lead Time – Weeks
- Expedite
- Large Wip
- Keep Everyone Producing
- Plant Layout by Function

NEW PARADIGM

- Produce Only What's Needed
- Lot Size as Reqd.
- Lead Time – Minutes
- Work to Schedule
- No Wip
- Be Productive
- Process Flow

know the suits, he'd said.

He was weaving his way around the stacks of work-in-process—"Good news," he thought. "That'll keep these guys busy until next year"—when he heard the big cutters fire up.

"All right!" he thought. "Back in business."

There is a persistent, nagging vision of the factory of the future, and it's a grim one.

The vision is expressed most eloquently in our popular culture, from Fritz Lang's 1926 film masterpiece *Metropolis*, with it's brooding, Gothic factories and drone-like workers, to the modern film *Batman*, where, once again, people seem an afterthought in the dark factories of the future. Since the beginnings of the Industrial Revolution, the factory of the future seems to have been moving toward a soulless place.

Even our optimistic visions have been of an increasingly automated future, a "lights-out" factory, humming quietly in the dark while the occasional human supervisor tiptoes in to read the meters.

We have seen, in both our optimistic and pessimistic visions, a factory of the future based on *hardware*. It is a peculiarly Western viewpoint to see the future in terms of next year's gadgets. It's also a peculiarly dangerous viewpoint for manufacturing, because it has led us to think that we can buy our way out of our problems.

We can't.

Remember Ross Perot's quote: "Brains and wits will beat capital spending 10 times out of 10."

Our vision of the factory of the future is built on the assumptions that lay beneath the factory of the present.

Let's look at the old paradigm:

1) Bigger is better. As long as you're running 1000, why not run another 3000? After all, they're practically free, aren't they? We can even calculate, scientifically, what the economic order quantity is supposed to be.

2) Long setup or changeover times are a given. But it really doesn't matter, since we're amortizing them

over a large number of units.

3) Lay out the factory by function. Put all the lathes in one place, all the blenders in another. Let the material travel around, sometimes for miles, to the department specializing in turning, blending or whatever, to get the optimum run.

4) More lead time is better. If we order materials earlier, we might get them on time.

5) The measure of productivity is noise and sweat. Keep all the equipment running and people busy all the time.

6) Stick to a rigid chain of command. The farther down in the chain you go, the less need there is to think.

7) Supervisors' roles are to think and keep people busy; workers' roles are to keep busy and don't think.

8) We do our capacity planning by visible backlog. If the stack of material around the equipment is growing, we must need more capacity. If the pile is going down, slow down.

9) Nobody believes the schedules. Expediting is justified as an act of flexibility or as a response to customer needs.

The old paradigm is built on the slippery slopes of *efficiency*. Efficiency is important, right? A more efficient factory is a more profitable factory. So it only makes sense to keep all the functional areas together—the lathes with the lathes, the blenders with the blenders—and make their operators high efficiency specialists. And it's equally important to know exactly how efficient those departments are. And we need to keep breaking departments down into smaller and smaller sub-departments and measure their efficiency. Thank heavens for computers! With a little luck and a lot of programming, we'll be able to tell you to the second when all the fat is in our direct labor.

Not that there's a lot of fat. Since the new automated machinery was installed, we've got three shifts running seven days a week to keep the machine utilization numbers up—you can tell the factory's productive just by the noise level. Inventory's piling up, but that's the point of warehouses. Big lot sizes mean low

The old paradigm is built on the slippery slopes of efficiency.

81

unit costs. In fact, bigger is better everywhere.

But is it really?

Let's look at the new paradigm for the factory of the future:

1) Make only as much as you need, not as much as you can.

2) Economic lot size is what is required by the customer, one or 1,000.

3) Eliminate steps and move to a more process flow.

4) Measure productivity by total hours and total cost incurred, not efficiency or utilization.

5) Lead times are *short*.

6) Schedules have credibility, and production fits the schedule.

7) Capacity requirements are visible.

8) Quality, flexibility and being on-time are the meaningful measurements of performance.

We've moved from a capacity-driven to a customer-driven environment.

As we've mentioned before and will mention again, in the last decade we've moved from a capacity-driven to a customer-driven environment. In our baseline industries—automobiles, machine tools, chemicals, textiles—the capacity to produce probably exceeds the total market demand for the product. In the automobile industry, for example, the *Wall Street Journal* recently put the over-capacity figure at a whopping 20 percent. The automobile industry could make 12 cars, but people only want to buy 10.

There is not any gadget, any high-tech machinery, any automation that can change a factory over from a capacity-driven outlook to a customer-driven outlook. It has less to do with the equipment we work with and more to do with the way we do things.

Many of the assumptions our manufacturing companies work under are not tied to a capacity-driven outlook and are, to a large extent, leftovers from the Industrial Revolution. For example, our obsession with seeing cost reduction solely in terms of driving down direct labor. When we focus on cost reduction, it tends to be a very narrow focus, and that focus is generally the shop floor. Which made sense when direct labor was the single largest element in our product cost.

Direct labor now typically makes up a much smaller proportion of product cost. In fact, in high-tech industries such as computers, direct labor can be as little as five percent of the overall costs. While it's true that manufacturing is a game of inches, not miles, it's also true that our critical resources are limited. So where do we put the brain power to help bring about cost reductions? In the area that represents five percent of the costs?

It's that kind of thinking that has led to some extremely poor decisions on automation. Even one of the most successful corporations in the world, IBM, has been stung by the automation bug. Two heavily automated factories failed to deliver the anticipated benefits, not because of a failure of automation, but because the products made by the factories didn't succeed in the marketplace, and the expensive dedicated equipment stood idle.

The anticipated benefits of the automation never materialized, because, in some cases, there was little point in spending a fortune to drive down direct labor costs. This is especially true when, as in IBM's case, we saw automation as a solution, rather than a problem-solving tool. Many of the robots and much of the automation were ripped out and the tasks replaced with thinking workers. The productivity improvements are impressive.

In the mid-1980s, GM spent $48 billion on capital improvements, mostly robots and automation, including building three highly automated factories from the ground up. The giant automaker was stunned when the automation didn't yield the productivity results they'd anticipated. Ford, which lacked the bucks for such a spending spree, concentrated on their culture, on quality and flexibility. The result?

The much smaller Ford consistently out-earns GM. Still in the auto industry, Chrysler chairman Lee Iacocca ruefully told *Fortune* that automation alone wasn't enough to guarantee quality and competitiveness.

"One of our most expensive and highly automated plants gives us the most trouble," he says.

Fortune, in fact, summed the problem up best:

"Old machinery can outperform new by a wide margin if the production system and the workers are well trained," wrote Kate Ballen. "Conversely, new equipment operated under archaic procedures may not boost productivity much at all."

The secrets of productivity are rooted in flexibility, speed and solving the million $20-problems.

"We identified our top priorities," Compaq Computer President and CEO Rod Canion told co-author Michael Bane, "and from a manufacturing standpoint— in fact, for several years now—we've identified responding to changing demands in the mix of products as a top priority of manufacturing. And so in trading off the different things they (manufacturing) do, they trade off in favor of flexibility. What that means is it probably costs you a little more to build the product. It means the way you set up things changes. It (flexibility) has an effect on other trade-offs. But if that's important to you, you have to adjust to meet it."

The result is that Compaq, one of the most successful companies in American business history, can quickly alter its product mix based on feedback from its large dealer base. The fact that the actual cost-per-unit rises is more than offset by greater sales achieved by meeting customer expectations.

Flexibility and speed even have strong quality implications.

"Doing it fast forces you to do it right the first time," says John Young, CEO for Hewlett-Packard.

Even our terminology, though, is a holdover from the Industrial Revolution. We think in terms of "direct" and "indirect" labor. In our graphic, "Run" is direct labor, the other activities indirect.

TRADITIONAL
FACTORY

VENDOR | Receive | Inspect | Move | Store | Issue | Queue | Set Up | Run | Move | SHIP

The implication of "indirect" is "unnecessary" or, even worse, inconsequential. Yet, realistically, the direct/indirect emphasis is totally false. It does not reflect how a product is really made—people who move material, people who record data, people who train new employees, people who do preventive maintenance of machinery are as necessary as the people who run machines. Direct labor is an *arbitrary* distinction, based largely on the activities in the factory that were easiest to measure.

Second, and most important, the direct/indirect labor emphasis has allowed us to concentrate on direct labor while accepting—or ignoring—the indirect labor component.

It took the Japanese, who suffered their own Industrial Revolution after World War Two, to change the terminology.

Instead of the false distinction of direct/indirect, the Japanese made the distinction between "value-adding" and "non-value-adding." In our graphic, inspection, move, setup, queue are all non-value-adding. In fact, *The Harvard Business Review* recently referred to the "hidden factory," the factory that moved, inspected, handled paperwork, issues—and ran up costs.

"...In the 'hidden factory,' where the bulk of manufacturing overhead accumulates, the real driving force comes from transactions, not physical products," wrote Jeffrey G. Miller and Thomas E. Vollmann. "These transactions involve exchanges of the materials and/or information necessary to move production along, but do not directly result in physical products."

The Harvard Business Review concluded, "Moreover, in today's environment, production managers have more direct leverage on improving productivity through cutting overhead than they do through pruning direct labor."

The concepts of value-adding and non-value-adding give us a powerful window on our processes and a tool to exercise that leverage.

In our Executive Management classes, we always ask whether anyone has worked at eliminating waste and reducing costs, and it always gets a laugh. Heck,

The direct/ indirect emphasis is totally false.

one CEO told us, he'd spent his whole *career* trying to eliminate waste and reduce costs!

But where do we focus our efforts? Traditionally, we've focused on direct labor as the area of our concern.

But let's think about value-adding and non-value-adding. Shouldn't we focus our waste-cutting, cost-reducing attentions on non-value-adding activities? Every elimination of a non-value-adding activity means an increase to the bottom line. Of course, we can't eliminate *all* non-value-adding activities—we need data records, maintenance and managerial help. But how many such activities can we minimize?

In fact, suppose we *institutionalize* that mindset? Suppose we challenge every activity, and keep on challenging them? That makes a lot of sense. Think of a manufacturing business the same way you'd think of the family house. While it might be cool to say, "If it ain't broke, don't fix it," that's not the way we actually work. We don't, for instance, ignore the house until the roof is falling in and rain is blowing through huge cracks in the wall. Since we know our home is a major, long-term investment that has a direct correlation on our standard of living, we perform preventive maintenance on it. We fix the roof before it's a total loss; we replace the siding before the wall caves in. In fact, don't we look around for ways to add value to our home? Maybe the traffic pattern in the kitchen is awkward. But we see that if we move the stove and open a new door, the kitchen will be a dream to cook in. Maybe we see that by extending the bedroom wall a few feet, what was previously wasted space can become a much-needed closet.

What have we lost by adopting this mindset?

Nothing. We've changed our mindset; it hasn't cost us a cent.

What have we gained?

In our house analogy, we've maybe reduced wasted space. We've also made our home more efficient by heading off problems before they happen, which means cost reduction.

We've gained an enhanced place to live, a higher

quality place. In a manufacturing environment, we've also gained quality, because, for the first time, we're starting to get down to the root causes of bad quality instead of just separating the good ones from the bad ones.

We've gained a quicker response time to our customers' expectations and demands, because we've streamlined our processes, allowing changes to happen more quickly and with less agony.

We've also, along the way, "invented" a process called Just-In-Time.

The very basis of Just-In-Time, or JIT, rests on the concept of *continuous improvement*, constantly challenging every activity to see whether it can be streamlined, changed for the better or, better yet, totally eliminated.

What we now think of as JIT grew out of Toyota Motor Corporation's system aimed at producing "only necessary items in a necessary quantity at a necessary time." On the surface, this is a little like saying you're going to the track and only pick the winners. Like the execs who say they've spent their entire careers trying to eliminate waste and reduce costs.

There are a number of tools and techniques to help us achieve more of a flow environment. Yet like our other powerful tool, automation, they must be used with care, and with a complete understanding of *why* that particular tool is being used at that particular time, and *what*, in fact, is really happening.

Consider the visual replenishing system called kanban. It has been met with much enthusiasm. However, kanban has been frequently confused with the whole of JIT, which, of course, it isn't. The word kanban, in Japanese, means symbol or sign board. In manufacturing, a kanban card is used to signal the previous workstation that more material is needed.

In a kanban system, sometimes called a demand pull system, material is, in effect, pulled through the line by demand. Central to the JIT concept of making only what's needed, the ultimate pull comes from the customer. This idea isn't particularly new or even Japanese. Not so many years back, when we wanted

Kanban has been frequently confused with the whole of JIT.

87

fresh milk, we put an empty milk bottle on our porch. The milkman saw the empty bottle and replaced it with a full one. Instant kanban. The milk bottle served as the kanban signal to let the milkman know the material—milk—needed replenishing.

Because it's a visual system, with cards or balls or empty bins or even milk bottles signaling the need for more material, it's easier to see at a glance what's really happening on the shop floor. Since the signal typically isn't given until you can see the materials are almost used up, the system has credibility. When the due date is on paper from a remote scheduling system, the credibility of the need is always subject to question.

Kanban works well...sometimes.

For kanban to really work well—or work at all— several prerequisites must be in place:

1) A firm rule to *not* produce more until the "customer" signals he or she is ready must be in effect

2) Very small lot sizes

3) Repetitious usage

4) Very few items

5) Very short lead times

6) Very few rejects

7) Excellent material planning

8) Excellent capacity management

When some companies put kanban into effect after meeting all the prerequisites, it was like a miracle! Speed was up! Quality was up! The whole process flowed smoothly.

That kanban was great stuff!

But was it the kanban technique or was it meeting the prerequisites that caused the impressive results? It was the prerequisites, of course. The process had been brought under control, simplified and constantly monitored.

Kanban was icing on the cake.

Of course, we want to produce what's necessary, and of course, we want enough at the right time. If we asked for a show of hands, we'd probably get something close to total agreement.

But is that what we really do? Remember our

graphic of the Traditional Manufacturing Process versus the Ideal Manufacturing Process?

TRADITIONAL TO IDEAL FLOW

FACTORY

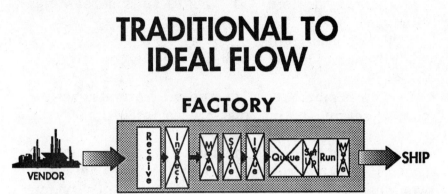

In the Ideal process, we've minimized and, where possible, eliminated non-value-adding activities, such as inspection and moving materials. We've also sped up the throughput time and reduced lot sizes.

Let's take a closer look at those lot sizes.

The Smaller Lot Size Surprise

As in our example at the beginning of the chapter, large lot sizes were (and, in many factories, still are) accepted as a given. In fact, we used to *certify* people in calculating Economic Order Quantities—remember those circular slide rules for "scientific" inventory management? At one time, they were considered state-of-the-art tools.

Why did we need those circular slide rules?

Because large lot sizes were a given.

But why were they a given?

The biggest single factor in large lot sizes is *mindset*.

We run large lot sizes because we've always run large lot sizes. Bigger is better is the old paradigm. And, after all, we're probably going to need more soon, so we might as well go ahead and produce them now.

There's an exercise that our vice president, John Civerolo, does in our World Class Performance For Managers class that's as telling as it is infuriating. John takes a lot size and then begins to whittle away on it. If the EOQ is 500, John will ask whether it has to be 500, or can it be 499? 498? 497? 496?

Usually, around 350, people start screaming, "Enough!"

They get the point.

Of course, there are other excuses for large lot sizes:

-The "Price Break" mentality. We amortize the cost of set-up, tooling, etc. over a large number of items.

-Long setup or changeover times are a given, something akin to death and taxes. Small lot sizes would also require frequent material issues, which would increase material transactions and handling.

-Our costing and measurement systems focus on minimizing unit costs and maximizing direct labor efficiency.

So why would we *not* want to run large lot sizes?

How about the fact that, in the ultra-competitive 1990s, carrying a large inventory makes about as much sense as changing your savings account into silver bars and burying them in your backyard. In both cases, you've got something of value, but you've got something with almost no flexibility. Excess inventory represents money tied up, unable to be put to work. Worse still are the "hidden" costs of inventory—storage space, losses, obsolete items/"write-downs," material movement charges, the cost of paperwork and other hidden costs. The result is that it takes more capacity today to produce what we hope is needed in the future. That capacity could perhaps be better utilized for products needed today.

Large lot sizes are also a tremendous impediment to quality.

Consider, for example, a case where a component is used in a finished product, and the product is produced at a rate of five per day, or 100 per month. Because of the relatively short run time and high setup time, it's not uncommon for the components to be produced in lots of 300, a three-month supply.

Suppose we produce 300, then use five for today's requirements, only to discover a major defect. Very

Large lot sizes are also a tremendous impediment to quality.

likely, we have 295 components with the same defect sitting in the stockroom. So what are we going to do? Make 300 new ones? Discover who is responsible so you can charge it to their budget? Or figure out a way to rig together the 295 bad ones? That's a no-brainer, right? How long do you want to remain employed at this place? The emphasis, you'll notice, is not on correcting the original quality problem, which means that, more than likely, the same problem will be repeated in the *next* 300, and we'll get to perform the same exercise again.

If we try to scrap 295 pieces, somebody is going to take a hit. If we'd made five pieces instead of 300, we'd only have to worry about scrapping a days-worth, not nearly as big a deal. We could focus our attention on what really caused the problem—the quality problem— and prevent it from happening again.

Often, the defective parts aren't discovered until more are used. Let's say we don't discover the problem until the customer complaints start rolling in, and we've used up half the 300 run. It may be months since the parts were produced, and it's pretty difficult to reconstruct what happened several months ago on the factory floor. We may never be able to track down the quality problem, which means there's a high likelihood of the problem recurring.

If the components we're using today were made yesterday, it's much easier to track down the problem and solve it. Since we're currently making the parts, we can immediately implement the proposed changes to solve the problems and find out immediately whether the solutions work.

The Question of Capacity

The issue of "make what you need" versus "make all you can" is a particularly vexing one. In our discussions with manufacturing executives about capacity, we routinely ask the following question:

If you are presently making 400 per week, you need 600 per week and you have the potential to make 900 per week, how many should you make? Fully 50 percent of the executives say, "Nine hundred, of course."

The old paradigm is that if you don't produce 900, you're not being productive, not minimizing cost. In addition, perhaps if you make more, maybe Sales can sell more.

The real issue, of course, is that you only need 600. Producing to the max is not necessarily the most productive; we only want to make what we need. What Sales can sell should have been decided in the planning process; otherwise, the Sales "plan" is most likely just a guess on what Manufacturing can produce.

Instead of random guesses, we need to measure productivity by how many hours and dollars it took to make what we needed, not how close we came to "full capacity."

One key to our success in manufacturing in the 1990s comes down to a simple equation:

Our demonstrated capacity (what we can make) must equal our required capacity (demand).

Let's look at demonstrated capacity. In a global customer-driven environment, total manufacturing capacity, in many cases, is greater than the market size. The capability of the equipment is just not in perfect balance with the demands of the product mix. If we produce to the max, what we used to think of as 100 percent "utilization," what we'll end up with is a warehouse (or many warehouses) full of inventory. Money tied up in inventory is not being used to develop new products or to keep existing product lines on the cutting edge of customer demand. The larger our inventory, the less flexible we are in responding to changing markets. We might have a modification or a new blend of a product that's more suited to the market, but we're not going to rush that modification or blend if we've got a year's supply of the original in the warehouse.

Ideally, in a World Class environment, we respond to our customers' expectations as opposed to expecting our customers to respond to us. Red Poling, the incoming chairman of Ford, recently pointed out that his challenge was how to manage a business where the

Producing to the max is not necessarily the most productive. . .

capacity for making cars far exceeds the demand for those cars. In the old days, we'd have just made as many cars as we could, producing to the max, secure in the knowledge that somebody would eventually buy all those cars.

That old world no longer exists.

To survive in the new world, flexibility is critical. But how can we be flexible if we don't know where we can flex? Flexibility requires having a clear vision of how much capacity is needed to meet demand—customer needs—then matching our demonstrated capacity to meet that need.

There are five panic-free steps to matching capacity to the customer needs:

1) Determine the required capacity

2) Measure the demonstrated capacity

3) Compare the demonstrated with the required capacity

4) Adjust the demonstrated capacity

5) Or, as a last resort, adjust the required capacity

The five steps to managing capacity are continuous. The first three can be supported with computers and formulas, but they are the easiest steps. The difficult steps are four and five, and they must be done by people. It's people who manage a business, and it's people who should be accountable for successful results.

Steps four and five are vital in closing the loop in the process and achieving "buy-in" to the schedules. By involving both the planners and the shop floor in steps four and five, ownership is transferred to those people. Finger-pointing ceases.

If the demonstrated is less than the required, we have a bottleneck. We have two options, two faucets we can turn. We can increase the number of scheduled hours, maybe add more employees or another shift, or we can increase the productivity of the hours currently scheduled.

Our future performance isn't locked into our past performance, but if, historically, we've been making 20 units a week, and our required capacity is 50 units a week, something has got to give. Doing more of the same will, most likely, produce more of the same results.

Our future demonstrated capacity is determined by multiplying the hours scheduled to work by the effectiveness or productivity of those hours.

Determining the effectiveness of those hours is tricky. Effectiveness (or productivity) is often incorrectly measured by machine utilization or efficiency. Some of the scheduled work hours are used for such non-value-adding activities as rework, scrap, equipment downtime, setup time, waiting for tools, absenteeism, answering technical questions, interpreting specs, reporting labor or material transactions, working around material shortages, moving material and general inefficiencies brought about by all of the above.

The bottom line is that as these "unscheduled" interruptions eat up the scheduled hours, less work gets done. Demonstrated capacity is reduced.

Historically, we thought low efficiency was primarily caused by poor work ethic—our people were lazy, had no pride, and basically didn't care. Notice that most of the inefficiencies are really caused by interruptions out of their control. Most of our inefficiency is the result of bad process, not bad people.

Traditional efficiency measurements usually evaluate effectiveness during the time the machine is humming or people are "clocked" in. Those measurements don't take into account the time spent on most non-value-adding activities. In fact, we've traditionally relentlessly ignored those non-value-adding activities, or actually institutionalized them by building them into the standards. The result is that we can have a department that's 100 percent efficient—both hours they worked!

Equipment or machine utilization traditionally measures the percentage of time we are trying to be effective, not how effective we really were. Demonstrated capacity in the past is what we have actually done. In the future, demonstrated capacity will be:

Scheduled hours X Productivity factor.

The productivity factor is calculated by dividing the actual quantity produced (sometimes expressed in

> **(Productivity) is often incorrectly measured by machine utilization or efficiency.**

standard hours) by the scheduled hours. Because the productivity factor is tied to the actual quantity produced, it measures our *true* effectiveness. It also helps us uncover the magnitude of the non-value-adding activities and focus on reducing them.

By finding the root causes of these non-value-adding interruptions and removing them, we not only increase the productivity factor—and the capacity—but we also reduce costs. Rather than creating the illusion of reducing costs by producing to the max, an effort to continuously improve the productivity factor will yield real cost savings. Fundamental quality improvement techniques such as brainstorming, pareto analysis, cause-effect diagrams, etc., can be applied to overcome the obstacles to removing the interruptions.

Continually monitoring the up or down trend in the productivity factor gives executive management the means to evaluate cost reduction performance without getting tied up in daily details. And improving the productivity factor isn't tied to any single acronym. We can work on cutting down scrap, a TQM function; on set-up times, a JIT function; on materials shortages, an MRP II function. Overcoming tool shortages, downtime and attitude problems don't fall under any one acronym, either. The objective is to concentrate on running the business better, not acronyms.

If we find the demonstrated capacity is greater than the required capacity, we have an opportunity. Instead of making more to keep everyone busy, or sending everyone home without pay, we have a number of excellent options.

We can use the excess capacity for preventive maintenance, for working on quality or productivity improvement ideas, or to cross-train employees, increasing our own flexibility. It's an opportunity to invest those surplus scheduled hours!

Because we are—or should be—customer-driven, let's look at capacity from our customers' perspective. Our customers don't care about our super-deluxe equipment or the number of hours worked. They care about getting our product. In fact, many companies

The productivity factor measures our true effectiveness.

today find the extra time can be used very productively. They build it into their capacity plans. In other words, on most days, all the work gets done by the end of the day.

If You Can't Wait...

"This ad is for those who can't wait," read a two-page advertisement in a recent computer magazine, placed by a company who suggested it could deliver. Why?

"Because our flexible manufacturing system can be reconfigured or expanded in a matter of hours to match our production mix to your demand..."

Traditionally, we only think about capacity when we don't have enough of it. Grow the factory. Add new workers. Build a building. In a slowdown, though, capacity planning becomes only slightly more interesting than repainting the floor. Yet excess capacity can be very costly if the excess resources are not effectively redirected.

If the demonstrated matches the required, the system is said to be in balance. But don't worry—it won't stay that way for long. Shifting product mixes, changes mandated by the customer, new competition and other blips in the marketplace all conspire to change the required capacity, putting our system off balance. And new people, new products, aging equipment and other factors all work to change the demonstrated capacity.

When the demonstrated capacity is less than the required capacity, the last resort is to adjust the required capacity, change the master schedule. Our product might go on allocation, with each customer getting a specified amount. Or the result might be the customer demand going unfulfilled. We have become a capacity-driven, not a customer-driven, company, and that's dangerous. In today's climate, few niches go unfulfilled for long.

Should we have to adjust down the required capacity, we need to go back and link to our financial system. There are probably solid financial considerations that led us to arriving at the required number in the first place. Those bottom line projections must be updated to the new reality if we want a real bottom line.

But keep this in mind: Jumping prematurely to Step 5 can lead to a thoroughly unpleasant Step 6...Update resume!

Hauling Out The Slop

In the traditional paradigm, there was a lot of slop in the schedules—nobody actually knew what the "real" need date was, which led to conversations like, "Just tell me what you really need and when you really need it."

We may still be shipping all our product on time, thanks to some expediters with good running shoes. But the process itself is out of control.

In the new paradigm, things get done on time not because they're hot, but because they're due. We recently visited a company that is approaching World Class performance levels, and we had the opportunity to ask one of the operators what happened when he couldn't meet the schedule? He didn't understand the question. *Not* meeting the schedule was never considered an option. Performance to schedule is equivalent to zero defects.

Another important aspect of the factory of the future is a reorganization of the factory floor itself. One of the outgrowths of traditional mass production is the grouping of machines by function—all the lathes in one place, all the broaching machines in another. Raw material came to the lathes for operations, then passed on to the next department—broaching—where it waited its turn. Each department was another "stop and wait and move." No one made a whole product, they just broached or honed.

In the new paradigm, things get done on time because they're due.

97

TRADITIONAL FACTORY LAYOUT
(Equipment Grouped in Departments by Function)

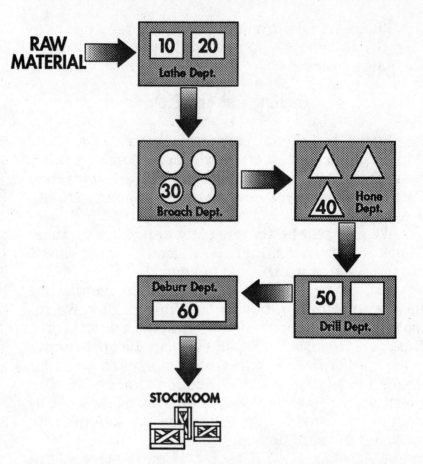

In the beginning, we did this to optimize the cost of performing each function. This sub-optimization approach did not look at the optimization of the whole process. We could, for instance, independently measure the efficiency of the lathe department. As our factories grew, and we added new products and options, we held on to the idea of functional departments, but bad things started to happen. The hidden factory emerged. We moved, stored and issued materials and subassemblies all over the factory! We turned moving materials into an art!

One of the side effects of all this shuffling was adding lead time to the overall process. It simply took longer to move the stuff around and a queue existed at every stop. Since the next operation couldn't always run the whole large lot size in a single day, or a single week, we checked partially finished materials back into the warehouse until we were ready to work on them. That action required part numbers and levels in the bill of material, plus transactions for tracking material in and out of the warehouse, plus additional people to handle all the paperwork and movements. Sometimes we built automated retrieval systems so robots, allegedly impervious to aggravation, could help us move material in and out of inventory more "efficiently." We didn't go after the fundamental problem, just tried to compensate for it. We even built scheduling systems to calculate due dates for each step.

Each one of these additional steps added how much value to the product?

Exactly none.

They did add a lot of cost, time and opportunity for quality problems.

Suppose, though, we stepped back and looked at how a product was really made. If lead times were reduced, and lot sizes were shrunk, could we come closer to the Ideal Process?

You bet we could.

Instead of moving materials all over the factory, it becomes feasible to regroup the equipment, putting all the machines that make a specific product together in a single work center, or *cell*.

FLOW FACTORY LAYOUT
(Equipment Grouped into a cell)

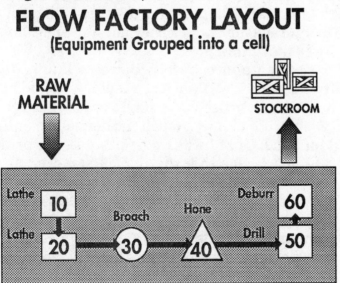

RAW
MATERIAL

STOCKROOM

Lathe 10
Lathe 20
Broach 30
Hone 40
Drill 50
Deburr 60

We have then dedicated a portion of the factory to a single item product or product family. Raw material now enters a cell, and each step is completed without delay or much movement. We would create factories within factories. Each small factory would focus on a single "product."

What are the advantages of such an arrangement?

1) For a start, we're not moving material all over the place, which reduces non-value-adding activities.

2) We reduce throughput time, the product flows quickly through the process, from raw material to finished product.

3) Thanks to faster throughput, we reduce the need for subassembles, their level in the bill, their spot in the high-rise automated warehouse, the inventory transactions to check them in and out of said warehouse.

4) We eliminate or reduce queues and work-in-process inventory.

5) Elimination of non-value-adding activities reduces or eliminates some overhead costs.

6) We have a more visual—hence, more credible—planning and scheduling system. It's hard to argue with the credibility of the system when you can see the person at the next machine running low.

7) Perhaps most important, we have more closely tied the people who make the product with the product itself. Once again, Daddy or Mommy can go home from work and explain what they do, take pride in what they do. They no longer run a screw gun for eight hours a day. They build things.

All of the above have a direct relationship on quality. In a work cell (or focus factory, i.e., a factory within a factory focused on a single product or product family) environment, it's much harder to let a quality problem slide. That has as much to do with pride as with the knowledge that the person standing next to you will bear the brunt of the problem.

Feedback of quality problems is instant and verbal. Accountability is isolated in the focused factory. Problems are caught before millions of pieces are run.

Work cell environments are ideally suited to au-

We would create factories within factories.

tonomous work teams.

As the new factory of the future takes shape, an interesting synergy starts happening. The advantages of mass production begin to disappear as the greater advantages of flexibility take hold.

In fact, we begin to approach a new Ideal Process: Raw material to customer, While-U-Wait. The bottom line of the flexible factory of the future is the ability to analyze our products with an eye toward meeting customer expectations. Do we really make cars, for example, or do we make frames, interiors, engines, etc., that are assembled to customer order?

As the new factory of the future emerges with focus factories capable of quickly making any item in any quantity the customer wants, it becomes increasingly more feasible to abandon several old paradigms. Maybe we shouldn't make anything to stock—totally eliminate the finished goods inventory. Keep inventory only in raw or a semi-finished stage where it is less expensive and much more flexible. If we have any finished goods, we don't need much if we can instantly replenish what was sold today. No more fire sales of obsolete products!

The investment to do it is peanuts.

The number of items to forecast and plan to produce (master schedule) can be significantly reduced while the quality and variability of the demand plans and factory schedules stabilize and improve. Planning and scheduling time is minimized, saving more money. Conventional order entry by end item and generating huge catalogues of confusing model-or SKU-numbers can be replaced with simple menu approaches. Fewer, simpler, easier to maintain bills of material and engineering documents are required. Traditional costing and pricing of every possible end item can be eliminated. All of this adds up to big savings in Sales, G&A, Engineering and overhead expenses. The investment to do it is peanuts. It does require thinking differently.

That future is not so far away. Here are two divergent examples:

In the hotly contested small computer market, several companies, including the enormously successful Dell Computing in Texas, assemble PCs to customer order. Sure, they make standard models, but you can have it your way. And you can have it your way as quickly as you can get the standard models.

Dell President and Founder Michael Dell is committed to that flexibility, and it has taken the company from a me-too clone-maker to a power within a tough industry.

One of the oldest mass-produced items in America is the handgun. Samuel Colt refined Eli Whitney's assembly line and concepts of standardized parts to begin manufacturing the Colt revolver before the turn of the century. Now, in the face of declining handgun sales and a radically changing marketplace, another firearm manufacturer, Smith and Wesson, has embarked on a radically new strategy.

Sure, they have a standard product line, but with a small minimum order, Smith and Wesson will make a gun your way, adding custom touches that were previously the province of expensive custom gunsmiths. S&W can now bring limited runs of specialized firearms to market quickly, filling niches as quickly as they are created. The result is that the venerable old company has now surpassed Colt in the worldwide market.

All these things bring us to another vision of the factory of the future.

The difference in the new factory of the future doesn't have that much to do with what you see. It's not a question of hardware or automation or electronic data exchange. Instead, it's a paradigm shift, a change in mindset—lots of focus factories and work cells, teams of people huddled together to solve problems, no work-in-process stacked around the machines, performance measurement by quality, not quantity. The new paradigm is leaner, meaner and faster to change when the customer demands it. And isn't that what we wanted to be all along?

DISCUSSION POINTS

1) Do you still use utilization and labor efficiency to measure productivity?

2) Do you measure the productivity factors and have on-going action teams to improve them?

3) Are you streamlining the product flow, eliminating steps and reducing lead times?

4) Do you have an aggressive program to identify and overcome the obstacles to smaller lot sizes? What progress has been made, and how do you measure it?

5) Has everyone been sold on the merits of reducing lead times and order quantities to a minimum?

6) What do you do with excess labor if the required capacity is less than the demonstrated capacity?

7) Review the five steps to managing capacity. Discuss how each step is currently done in your organization.

8) What are the key measurements for gauging factory performance? Do they motivate the factory to meet customer expectations?

9) Are the schedules on the plant floor valid; is performance to schedule measured and followed? Do you have informal systems, hot lists and multiple schedules that override the formal schedule?

10) Discuss the impact of short lead times and smaller order quantities on:
   a) making product to forecast versus making or finishing to customer order
   b) inventory levels
   c) forecasting and master scheduling
   d) order entry
   e) cost to create and maintain engineering documents and bills of material
   f) costing systems
   g) plant floor layout and methods

CHAPTER 7

Putting The Brakes On Chaos

"Sales and operations planning?" shrugs Bob Potter, Feel Good, Inc.'s CEO. "We already do that stuff." He was, in fact, getting a little sick of hearing about it. He'd hauled in a consultant on the subject last month, and nobody thought they heard anything new.

In another part of the building, Sales is in the middle of a special promotion on a soon-to-be-ready new product, buy three, get one free. They're also bidding on a big contract that'll mean $20 million of extra business above the plan if they get it. Chances look pretty good. Of course, District Sales Manager Pam Strong is beside herself with joy—she gets a sliding scale bonus if she exceeds her sales plan.

Meanwhile, Manufacturing has heard rumors of a "big order," but, hey, there's always rumors. Nobody in sales thought to mention the special promotion. Manufacturing is already under the gun from management; they've been told to cut inventory by 25 percent. Lowering safety stock is the tactic of choice. Ken Rich, the VP of Manufacturing just returned from a week-long seminar on how to reduce cost and improve machine utilization. He's convinced he can reduce the work force by 12 percent through attrition and simultaneously keep machines busy on both shifts. It's just a question of getting Production Control to release more work.

Distribution gets wind of the special promotion, so they decide to open up a warehouse on the West Coast to meet the anticipated demand. Of course, Manufacturing is traditionally late and partially ships warehouse orders, so Distribution VP John Morgan solves that by ordering more than he will sell over the next six months.

Engineering is excited about their new product, cutting edge all the way. Although, of course, it looks like it's going to be a quarter or so late, not what they told Sales. So what? There's no hurry, special promotions or anything like that.

The President and CFO are happy and excited, since they met with a Wall Street analyst and projected a 20 percent increase in the next quarter, primarily due to an exciting new product about to be released...

Everyone in business has plans, right? In 20 years of teaching classes, we've never had a company come in and say they didn't have some sort of planning for demand and capacity.

And that traditional thinking extends to companies outside our classroom door. If there is, in fact, a slogan for the last century of American manufacturing, it's probably "Somebody has a plan."

But do they?

Obviously, Feel Good, Inc., did. In fact, the old paradigm, as represented by Feel Good, Inc., was one of compartmentalization. There wasn't a single plan; there were *lots* of plans, and they weren't connected to each other. Bruce Achenbach, vice president of Trane, puts it best when he describes Trane's old planning process:

"I'd have a meeting with my Marketing VP," he says. "Then go down the hall and have a meeting with the Sales VP. Later, I'd talk to the Manufacturing guys, and they'd say something I'd jot down to mention to Marketing. Except, I'd get busy, and the item would never get mentioned. I was like a quarterback who, instead of going into a huddle, talked to each player individually."

But we *thought* the planning process was taking place! We thought all the individual plans were working well—after all, product did go out the door every month.

In fact, the formal planning process was *not* working. An informal, profit-draining system was in place and creating a false illusion.

The old paradigm looks something like this:

1) We believed the planning process was in place and working.

2) Everybody, independently, had a plan.

3) The plans were not linked, creating little islands of planning.

4) Nobody believed the other guy's plans, anyway.

5) Assigning accountability for meeting the invalid plans was a joke.

6) We made changes without regard to the overall consequences to the organization.

7) Planning was a top-down function with little ownership or buy-in at the lower levels of the organization.

The new paradigm is radically different:

1) There is a single integrated company game plan developed with an effective Sales and Operations Planning (SOP) process.

2) The plan is reviewed frequently and revised based on shifts in the marketplace.

3) The detail schedules and plans are based on flawless data.

4) Schedules are based in reality and linked tightly to the business objectives.

7) Flawless performance to the plan is the norm, not the exception.

"Changing to team play by the CEO and his immediate staff is what the SOP process is all about," says Charles M. Heineman, vice president of Ashbrook-Simon-Hartley. "It requires mutual understanding, trust and energy from all the players on the team. 'Turf' issues or apathy will destroy the effectiveness of the team, or a player."

'Turf' issues or apathy will destroy the effectiveness of the team, or a player.

The old paradigm assumes that all the plans are connected, all the gears are linked. Through the filters of the paradigm, we looked at the myriad plans and assumed they were working—after all, product was being shipped, wasn't it? In fact, the planning process was a shambles.

There are several basic reasons that traditionally structured planning doesn't work well:

1) The manufacturing plan isn't integrated with the financial plan, the sales demand, distribution requirements, special promotions and the like.

2) The detail plan that drives manufacturing is based on data that is not correct, such as mistakes in the bill of material or the inventory records.

3) Most plans are developed as open-loop systems— that is, there's no feedback. The result is dozens of different plans, black books, chalkboards and other informal systems.

4) There's not enough detail in the plans.

5) The plans are not updated frequently.

6) Because of Points 1-5, most of the plans lack credibility, lack accountability for meeting them, and the result is a process out of control.

We simply can't afford to blindly pump out products and assume we can sell them.

It's important to grasp early on the difference between the SOP process and the Annual Operating Plan (AOP). The annual operating plan is a once-a-year event, essentially a *snapshot* of the SOP process at a single point in time. As you go through the SOP process, you keep comparing it against the annual operating plan.

As long as the market was capable of absorbing everything we could produce, the penalty for not having integrated plans was not so severe. The need for a high quality demand plan to drive manufacturing wasn't as critical. We just cranked the factory up full steam, because we could sell as many as we could make. And the extra costs to compensate for poor quality got buried in overhead, SG&A, and was passed on to the customers.

But a customer-driven environment is more dynamic and cost competitive—the market is constantly shifting, and we simply can't afford to blindly pump out products and assume we can sell them, using inflation as the excuse for a price-increase. Today's customer-driven market is demand-limited, not capacity-limited, so emphasis shifts to making only as much as you need, not as much as you can. If you're only going to make what you need, it then follows that *knowing* how much you need is critical. And the customer-driven market offers the customer more choices, further complicating the decision of what to make.

Look at the state of the U.S. auto industry just a few years ago—they were producing lots of cars. It just so happened that no one was buying them. When Lee Iacocca took over Chrysler, there were Chryslers stashed in parking lots and warehouses all over Detroit. Keep making 'em, the old powers-that-were said, because that's efficient. They were still in the old capacity-driven paradigm, and it drove them to the very brink of extinction.

A customer-driven environment is also more of a niche environment. The market is more competitive. There are more options for the customers to choose from, and customers are—not surprisingly—more choosy. It's not enough, an executive of a major candy company told us recently, to make chocolate bars. They have to make chocolate bars in a wrapper with hearts on it for Valentine's Day, switch to flag packaging for the Fourth of July and add goblins for Halloween.

The implications of that simple statement for manufacturing is tremendous.

The last thing in the world the candy maker needs is a trainload of candy bars with little hearts on the wrapper on February 15. Like the space shuttle, the candy maker has a narrow "launch window" for the Valentine's Day chocolate bars. Missing the window potentially means losing a lot of money, or, worse, driving your customers into the waiting arms of your competition, who happened to hit the right window.

Since everybody has a plan, how do we know if our planning isn't working correctly?

There are six warning signs:

1) Shipping 60 percent of the monthly budget in the last week of the month.

2) Lots of inventory, but lots of shortages.

3) Lots of expediting—Hot Lists.

4) A lot of "finger-pointing."

5) Multiple bills of material.

6) Frequent physical inventory.

Any combination of two or more of the above is a clear sign of the disease.

A customer-driven environment is also more of a niche environment.

We take a physical inventory because our records aren't accurate. Aunt Molly looked in the kitchen pantry because she needed to know how much sugar she had. Aunt Molly, Inc., has the same need to know how much sugar is in stock, and one way to answer that question is to go out into the warehouse at each factory and count the bags.

The result is at that exact instant in time, we flatly know how many bags of sugar we have. We've also closed down the plant to find out that information, and the people we're paying to count the bags of sugar aren't doing what they're supposed to be doing, which is make product. And the next day—or even the next hour—the records are no longer accurate. We didn't fix any of the problems causing inaccurate records (i.e., poor data quality).

Aunt Molly had to have a recipe, remember, to tell her how to make the peppermint candy. That recipe, or bill of material, was critical, because the peppermint candy had to have the same taste every time—that's what the customers want. Customers expect to get the same product each time they buy, whether that product is peppermint candy or stealth bombers. But sometimes the recipe gets changed, altered, updated, revised. The result is multiple recipes, new bills of material. Plans based on inaccurate data are inaccurate—a quality problem, remember.

Manufacturing becomes life by hot list—forget the plan, which nobody believes anyway. Informal systems evolve. What do we absolutely, positively have to make to meet our latest customer order? Or which order do we have enough of the right material around to produce and make the financial numbers this quarter? Every month brings different surprises. Inventories build up. Shipments are late. Cash flow dries up.

The most conspicuous byproduct is a lot of "finger-pointing." All these surprises must be someone's, or someone else's, fault.

Also not surprisingly, we start building finished goods inventory. Some of that inventory consists of goods we manufactured that our customers don't want—we made the wrong product, so we'll just store it until somebody wants it. And since we're not sure what we need to ship, maybe we'd better make some extra "just in case." Some contracts or customer orders are run ahead of schedule, while others run late.

And it's good that we have the extra since, come the end of the month, we're going to have to take them apart and rebuild or repackage them into products we can ship!

Look at the Big Gears graphic.

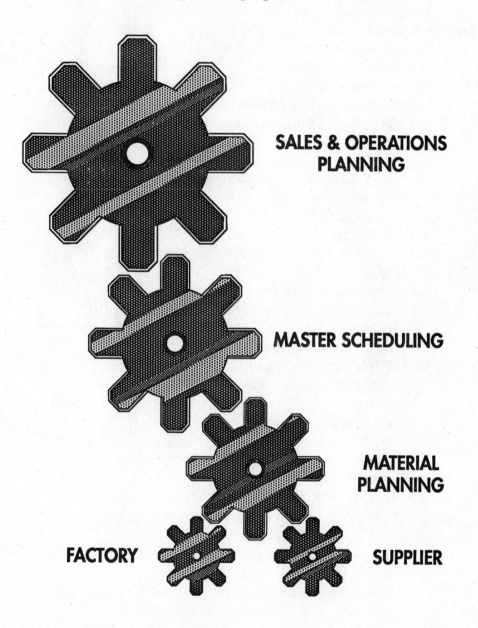

**SALES & OPERATIONS
PLANNING**

MASTER SCHEDULING

**MATERIAL
PLANNING**

FACTORY   **SUPPLIER**

We all understand mechanical advantage—a small turn of the big gear results in rapid turns of the little gear. The plan is the big gear, and when we crank it just a little, the factory and supplier gears spin a lot.

When the big gear spins a lot, when the plan does a lot of changing, the little gears spin like crazy. When we keep moving the big gear back and forth—turning up the steam, then turning down the steam—the small gears take a tremendous beating. And we all know that even the best gears don't last forever. They wear out or the teeth break off or the gears get disconnected.

We often find the gears are not connected at all.

Sadly, what we often find is that the gears are not connected at all. They spin independently of each other. Go back to our opening story. Sales, Manufacturing, Distribution and Purchasing didn't have a hint of what the other was doing. Money was being spent, critical resources committed, and who was in control?

No one.

Who knew what was actually going to happen?

No one.

By contrast, let's look at Bently Nevada. In 1976, before the advent of an effective SOP process driving their MRP II system, Bently Nevada made a list of its problems:

-Manufacturing lead times 16-26 weeks
-Manufacturing delivery promises unreliable
-A large portion of Sales/Marketing's day spent on delivery problems
-High inventories of the wrong products
-Manufacturing priorities wrong
-Difficult to get commitments from Manufacturing as to when an order will ship
-New product introduction takes a year or more
-More and more money "thrown" at Manufacturing problems.

In 1988, Bently Nevada went back to the problems, totaled the score and saw how well they'd done:

-Typical lead times six to eight weeks
-90-plus percent delivery promises made on time
-Sales time now focused on selling
-Inventories down, inventory turns up 3.8 to 6.0, product mix problems rare

-Sales determines priorities for using manufacturing
 resources
-Firm, reliable customer delivery commitments from
 Manufacturing within hours
-New products available within weeks of release
-Productivity up 400 percent, 1976-1988.
Impressive results, and they have continued to
improve.

Making The Gears Mesh

We are moving toward a customer-driven business—producing only what the market needs, no extras.
If we're going to produce what the market needs, it
certainly implies that we know what the market needs.
    But do we?
    How do we figure out what the customer wants?
Well, one executive told us recently, that's why God
created the Sales Department. All companies have
some kind of sales forecast. The only issue is who does
it, how much detail and how often it is updated. Even
contract, make-to-order, specialty businesses have
forecasts. They just don't get down to specific product
configuration forecasts.
    In the old paradigm, the Sales Department usually
comes up with a forecast in dollars for the coming
year.
    That information is often based on historical data,
and no small amount of arm-twisting to meet the desired
revenue plan. We sold $100 million last year; the
economy looks pretty good, so we ought to sell $110
million this year. The $110 million number then gets
batted to Manufacturing, who assures everyone that,
yes, they can make 80,000 units, if Sales manages to sell
them. And they hope the 80,000 units will create $110
million and be the right mix.
    But let's look at what has really happened. More
often than not, the salesmen have some kind of incentive
structure. If they sell more than the quota, they get a
bonus. Salesmen aren't stupid. If your income is based
on exceeding the plan, and what you want is a steady
income, you're going to have to have a plan of your own.

Now, from a salesman's financial viewpoint, does it make more sense to have the sales quota set high or low? Or, putting the question another way, would you like to make more or less money this year than last?

So the sales forecast, from the beginning, is often a hedged bet.

Manufacturing isn't stupid, either. They know that the sales forecast is low, but how low? Manufacturing now has to make a "best guess" as to how many units they're really going to have to make. Manufacturing also knows that if sales go sour, the Sales Department is likely to launch a discount special or some sort of incentive to purchase immediately, and that's going to put even more pressure on the already strained capabilities. The Controller might also mandate a "cut the inventory" directive, which also puts the organization into a tailspin.

The result is that sales forecast meetings too often resemble a back-room poker game, with all the boys puffing cigars and studiously keeping their cards hidden.

It's no wonder the gears don't mesh.

What we need to do is think more in terms of sales *planning*, as opposed to sales *forecasting*. Forecasting is waiting for orders; planning is aggressively going after those orders, having a specific set of detail plans and accountability for making the plans happen.

And more likely than not, the move from forecasting to planning is going to require a change in the compensation system for Sales. It's not that drastic a change, but it is one that has to be based on trust. Instead of paying a bonus for exceeding the plan, the sales bonus could be paid for *meeting* the plan. And we need to start integrating the salesmen's knowledge into our planning process and then tying compensation to the quality of the plan. Remember, the salesmen have a plan, even when we think they don't. We need that knowledge to improve the quality of the demand plans.

The Planning Moment

Real planning begins when we coordinate our sales plan with our manufacturing capabilities, which is what we mean by Sales and Operations Planning. SOP is not a meeting or a series of meetings; not a technique; not a computer report.

It is, rather, a *process*.

The SOP process looks at total demand and capabilities and helps align, or balance, the two. The demand may come from anticipated customer orders or contracts, actual customer orders, replenishing warehouse needs, interplant requirements or a combination of all these elements.

The SOP process always has to balance the basic constraints of people, time and money, and there are few absolutes.

There are five basic steps to successfully launching the SOP process:

1) Gather the data. This means summarizing historical and future demand plans, manufacturing plans, plus inventory and backlog by manufacturing product family in units and dollars.

2) Begin the sales planning process. This includes reviewing performance, the plan versus the actual; determining future customer needs, developing sales plans, defining inventory and backlog targets and running preliminary sales/operations plans.

3) Begin the production planning process. Again, we compare prior production plans to the actual. We check out capacity plans, the demonstrated versus the required capacity. We develop a new production plan, factoring in people, equipment and capabilities, then run a preliminary SOP.

4) Have the Partnership Meeting. Here's where we start putting the gears together. We bring together managers from Manufacturing and Sales/Marketing. Finance, Engineering, Human Resources and Purchasing are also represented. We identify conflicts, obstacles and critical issues. Alternative plans are considered and solutions to the obstacles are suggested. Then we put together the preliminary set of SOP plans.

Note that at this point we've gotten buy-in—it's no longer Sales' plan or Manufacturing's plan or Finance's plan. It's *the* plan. We've put together a horizontal partnership with people across the functional departments of the company who are going to be responsible for executing the plans. It's no longer a top-down directive.

5) Have the SOP Meeting. Key executives attend—in fact, the meeting should be chaired by the GM, President or the company's top operating officer. This is where the obstacles, conflicts and consequences to the alternatives are discussed and resolved. After considering the alternatives, executive management makes the decision. We've then created a vertical partnership, with top management who is responsible for running the business down through line managers who must make the plans happen. Ownership is now up and down and across the organizational chart.

Gearing Down

Let's go back to our gears graphic. We've solved the problems with the big gear—through the SOP process we've gotten it turning in one direction at a steady RPM. But the process still isn't under control. We've got to make sure the linkages between the big gear and the small gears—factory and suppliers—are in place.

That is, we want everyone working to the same plan. The plan tells us exactly what to make, and the challenge becomes communicating that plan to a detail level—the PC board stuffers at Feel Good, Inc., need to be stuffing the PC boards that go into the same products that executive management is basing revenue and profits on.

That seems a little self-evident, doesn't it? Under the old paradigm, though, that's not the way business worked. Under the old paradigm, schedules that were fairy tales were acceptable. Schedules hit the plant floor that were late before we even started. Since the schedules didn't tell us what we really needed to make, we made the easy items. Why not? At least efficiency was good.

Since the big gear was not connected all that tightly to the small gear, we might not even know exactly what we needed to make, so how could we know what material we needed to make it? As a result, we ordered a lot of everything, stacked it up somewhere and figured we'd use it up eventually. "Coverage"—keep something of everything on order—was the unwritten rule of the survivors.

In the new paradigm, we have to communicate specifics—what do we need to make, what do we have in inventory, what does it take to make it and what do we need to purchase? Another old friend and mentor, the late Oliver Wight, called this "the universal manufacturing equation."

This was easy when we were talking about Aunt Molly's kitchen. But as we got larger, as Aunt Molly became Aunt Molly, Inc., the simple mass of data, the volume of calculations and number of people who needed to know the information threatened to overwhelm us. We began coming up with all manner of informal systems, black books and the like, to answer the basic questions in the manufacturing equation. It took the computer, with it's ability to crunch numbers, to help us out of this bind.

What if we created a computerized system to help communicate the overall plan down the line and break it into detail? That's great, except there's a couple of catches. Computers, of course, can't do our thinking for us. They're just slick adding machines. If we want the computer to help us, we need to give it accurate data. The cliche is, "Garbage In; Garbage Out," and it could not be truer. Aunt Molly says it takes a cup of sugar and two cups of water to make 100 lemon drops. Let's say Aunt Molly, Inc., wants to make two million lemon drops. Due to a "bill of material" error, the recipe information ends up in the computer as "slightly" incorrect, maybe not as much water as required. With less water, instead of making two million lemon drops, the flawed bill of material yields a single two-ton lemon drop. Big difference.

When Aunt Molly was making her own lemon drops, if she ran out of sugar, she had the option of running to the 24-hour convenience store for more. On a run of two million lemon drops, Aunt Molly, Inc., is in deep trouble if, at the last minute, they discover there's no sugar in the warehouse. Also, when we talk in terms of two million lemon drops, or a three-million month, what does that mean to a guy on the wrapping line? To someone in Purchasing? Nothing! They need to know specifics—how many wrapped in red or how many cartons with hearts.

So we need a computerized system, based on very accurate data, to help calculate and communicate the detail plans—what everyone needs to be doing—throughout the organization. The information needs to be accurate and updated often. The resulting schedules need to be stable as well, since it's harder to meet a moving target.

We have a name for this system. It's called MRP II. MRP II is not a software program. It doesn't make any difference whether our product is simple or complicated, made to order or made to a forecast, an automobile or sugar syrup. MRP II still applies.

MRP II has had a profound effect on industry, and with good reason. Parts shortages, or the inability to ship product because of parts shortages, has plagued American industry for decades:

Wall Street Journal, 1978: "The Big Three auto makers spend more than $100 million a year to ship parts by air; the companies require the expensive, unscheduled air service when...poor production planning threatens to close an assembly line for lack of critical parts..."

Associated Press, 1983: "GM, which planned to assemble 318,000 cars in the month of August, instead will assemble about 280,000 due to component shortages..."

Wall Street Journal, 1983: Wall Street analysts estimate that GM lost the chance to earn an additional $200 million in the quarter because of parts shortages at assembly plants..."

Atlanta Journal-Constitution, 1984: "Lockheed-Georgia's failure to stock enough of one tiny part for its C-130 refurbishing program resulted in 91 workers being laid off Thursday..." (The part was a self-locking nut, by the way).

Wall Street Journal, 1984: "Kaypro Corp. said, 'there is a substantial possibility' the portable computer maker may be missing several million dollars in inventory...By June, inventories of parts had swelled to $66 million—several times the company's historic level. The inventory growth forced Kaypro to house electronic gear under a tent and in rented trailers..."

Wall Street Journal, 1987: "Mack Trucks Inc., Allentown, PA, said it expects to incur fourth-quarter losses because of continuing parts shortages that have prevented completing trucks on schedule..."

Wall Street Journal, 1988: "At the back of the sprawling factory, huge diesel engines are stacked against the wall, waiting for missing parts..."

MRP II provides the mechanism to link the gears. It provides the ability to take the business plan and break it down into the appropriate detail plans. Because the market, the data and the product are constantly changing, MRP II is a process to help manage change. At Bently Nevada, for example, they don't have a master scheduler; they have a master re-scheduler. It is a fluid, dynamic—and necessary—process.

The computer has given us the power to quickly and accurately handle the number crunching and information distribution necessary to MRP II.

The SOP process gives management a handle on the business and becomes the single most influential element in the MRP II process. Mismanage the SOP process, and the MRP II process will create the *wrong* plans, in detail, at the speed of light.

What It Isn't

The SOP process doesn't come about because someone in Sales talked to someone in Engineering on the way to the cafeteria. It doesn't come about when everyone in the company talks about the plan, but not in the same room.

The SOP process must be a formalized one, and it

must be a process that has the unconditional support of the people at the top. A formal SOP policy clearly spells out how the process is to be performed and who is responsible for what is mandatory. This policy sets the ground rules for how we balance market demand, company resources and financial objectives.

The new paradigm calls for us to create a single, integrated game plan, to understand why it's important to us and to respect it.

The new paradigm also calls for buy-in, ownership of the plan at all levels. Obviously, that can't be mandated from the top down. The Partnership Meetings are particularly vital to pushing ownership of the plan throughout the company, to create consensus. There's no way people in the company can respect and trust the plan unless it's *their* plan.

Otherwise, it's just gears spinning.

"There's no magic in the SOP process," wrote Robert E. Agan, president of Hardinge Brothers, Inc. "It simply takes what common sense tells us is the correct way to interface all the various functions of a business and provides us with a regimented means to get the job done. It provides a common ground where issues can be raised and responded to by all functions of the organization."

He went on to say that Hardinge is sold on the SOP process.

"It's not easy. It takes time and commitment. It takes attention and education. But the benefits are obvious."

In Total Quality Management (TQM), the first step is to bring the process under control.

The "process" of purchasing material and converting it to salable product also needs to be under control. We need everyone working on the right things in the right quantity at the right time. Everyone in every organization is willing to comply. Their next question is what are the right items, right time and right quantity? That question we often hear from the plant floor—"What do you *really* need and when do you *really* need it?"—is a clear sign that the process is *not* under control.

It's simple in concept, but, like many other points in the manufacturing business, difficult in execution.

As we move toward increased flexibility, it becomes even more difficult. The situation becomes more fluid—we are responding to our market, our product mix changing. We are pushing to bring new products to market more quickly. Our planning becomes at the same time more critical—we can no longer afford to waste critical resources—and harder to do.

The concept of a time fence helps us visually see our flexibility to respond to demand changes.

MANAGING SCHEDULE CHANGES

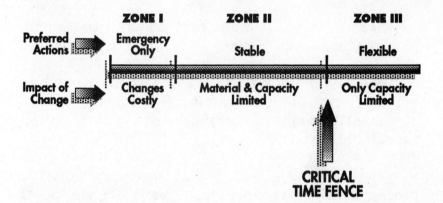

Early in the picture, there is an area where the plan is frozen—to change the plan inside this fence would mean a substantial commitment of resources. A second, larger area allows change, but with constraints. Finally, out on the horizon, change is allowed without constraint. Demand changes may occur any place in the time horizon, but adjusting the manufacturing plan is another question.

What we want to do is shrink the critical area where we can't make changes in the plan. This means a focus on shrinking our manufacturing and supplier lead times. In the meantime, not living within the time fence constraints causes chaos and lost profit.

DISCUSSION POINTS

1) Discuss how the five steps in the SOP process are currently done. Identify weaknesses.

2) Is an SOP policy written, agreed on and followed?

3) Do key executives attend monthly SOP meetings, or is attendance delegated down in the organization?

4) Do sales compensation plans help or hinder getting high quality demand plans?

5) Are financial plans derived from the manufacturing and sales plans?

6) Do you track performance for the sales and manufacturing plans in meaningful product groups? Is actual performance conforming to expectations within acceptable variation?

7) What are the time fences for each product or process family? Do changes to the manufacturing plans consider the time fences?

8) Are the detail schedules for the purchase and manufactured items valid? Are these schedules derived from SOP plans—are all of the gears engaged? Are they formally communicated to the people who buy or make the items?

9) Do you have a periodic audit of the quality of inventory records and bills of material? Does the accuracy conform to minimum expectations?

10) How frequently do you have material, purchased or manufactured, shortages? What are the root causes of the shortages?

Clout is Out

It started with the board, or maybe the bid.

Before the problem, Sheila Hood, the Purchasing Manager of Feel Good, Inc., had been pretty pleased. Their newest product, the Super Analyzer, was scheduled to come on line next quarter, and the factory would be ready to roll in a few months. Of course, nobody had bothered to tell her until she'd overheard an engineer talking about the new product in the cafeteria. Damned engineers! One of the engineers told her he'd actually called a supplier to ask about parts. Called one of her suppliers! The nerve! Who did they think she was—a clerk?

The regular suppliers were miffed to be lumped into the overall bidding, but hey, it's a tough world. In fact, the regulars were going to have to pony up a little extra, cut their bids to the bone, on this one. After all, they made a lot of money off Feel Good, Inc., didn't they?

What really burned Hood, though, was that the first batch of Super Analyzer PC boards just came in from the lowest bidder, and Manufacturing went through the ceiling. The physical size of the board—actually, just one small corner—was about three millimeters too large to run through the new automated machinery. When she'd called the supplier, he was patronizing enough to really make her mad. She'd come up through QA, and if he wanted hard-line, she'd give him hard line. The next time he dealt with her, he'd think he'd been struck by lightning.

It's not his fault that her Engineering Department can't come up with clear specs. Besides, he countered, hadn't he cut Feel Good, Inc. a deal? So maybe Feel Good, Inc. had to do a little culling. It happened. Besides, he pointed out, the EOQ was pretty big, so sorting the good from the bad shouldn't be any

---

SUPPLIERS

OLD PARADIGM

- Clout & Leverage
- Price Breaks and Large Quantities
- Multiple Sources
- Focus on Purchase Price
- LT in Weeks/Months
- Purchasing Dept. Solely Responsible

NEW PARADIGM

- Partnerships
- Frequent Deliveries
- Single Sources
- Focus on Total Purchase Costs
- LT in Days
- Total Company Effort

big deal, should it? If she didn't have to do all this running around, she thought, she could concentrate on doing her job—get out a crate of bids and really save some money!

She was thinking about re-bidding the whole thing, but only after taking the Engineering Department on a tour of the factory so they could see how some of the products were made.

Still, Hood thought, taking her sixth aspirin of the morning, she was pretty close to making her favorable purchase price variance numbers for her bonus. Maybe it wasn't all bad...

What's your definition of an ideal supplier? The answers we get look something like this—an ideal supplier:

1) Delivers on time
2) Gives frequent deliveries
3) Sells at a reasonable price
4) Needs a minimum of paperwork
5) Has quick response
6) Delivers defect-free material that doesn't have to be inspected
7) Offers technical assistance and ideas to improve the item

How many suppliers would be willing to do all of the above? The answer is *all of them*. Every company feels they already strive to meet these requirements. And we are all suppliers. So the question becomes why aren't suppliers living up to those seven expectations today?

The best answer we've heard comes from Hewlett-Packard's Manufacturing Specifications Manager Dan Marshall, who led H-P's on-time procurement improvement.

"Our study clearly revealed that *communications* was the chief culprit in on-time delivery failures," he says. "Hardly a popular conclusion, since it made us a primary cause of the problem."

Simply put, the customer—not the supplier—is most often the problem. Yet, that doesn't fit the old paradigm.

Relationships with suppliers in the past have stopped just short of total warfare. The word of the day was C-L-O-U-T—"I'm the customer and you're the supplier; when I say, 'Jump!,' you just ask how high..." Companies have tried to realize benefits by exercising clout and leverage over their suppliers.

Inc. magazine reported a few years back that "the warehousing business in Detroit has never been so good since companies went to JIT." We didn't fix any problems, just shoved them back to the supplier and mislabeled it "JIT." Problems like these are not the result of a faulty system, but of a failure to communicate what we're doing to our suppliers.

Under the old paradigm, we defined "communication with suppliers" as our Purchasing agent going out to lunch once a year with the supplier and threatening them. That's not the communication we have in mind. This is the way we've dealt with our suppliers in the past:

1) We dealt with suppliers through a bidding process. The low bidder got the job, regardless of whether it was a new supplier or an old supplier. Shop around for today's best deal.

2) The most frequent route to price reduction was to purchase large lot sizes to get the price break. We only considered the purchase price of the material, not the total costs such as additional cost for storage, moving and the like.

3) We intentionally developed multiple sources for the same item, allowing us to play one supplier off against the other. We maneuvered to get clout, and we used it like a big stick at every chance we got.

4) We kept our suppliers in the dark as much as possible, lest they tell our competitors some damaging information.

5) We accepted lead times as a given, since we were all lying to each other about when we needed the material anyway. More lead time is better was the unstated policy. If we weren't sure whether the lead time was six or eight weeks, we opted for 10 weeks. Ordering earlier gave us greater comfort that the odds of getting it on time would increase.

We accepted lead times as a given.

Supplier lead times are often the major factor limiting our flexibility.

6) The supplier was the enemy. Every penny we beat the supplier out of was a penny in our pocket.

7) Because the supplier was our enemy, we needed lots of inspection to catch the bad material they were always trying to pawn off on us, and we needed lots of paperwork to make sure that everyone's behind was covered.

8) Suppliers were the sole province of the Purchasing Department, and you risked Purchasing's wrath if you even so much as said hello to a supplier.

9) Supplier performance was a Purchasing Department problem—that's what they got paid to do.

The situation is so critical that the 1989 book, *Made In America: Regaining The Productive Edge*, from the prestigious MIT Commission on Industrial Productivity, listed better relationships with suppliers as a vital strategy for industry in the 1990s.

"Cooperate with suppliers rather than treating them as adversaries," the authors of the study wrote. "To achieve this end, firms must establish long-term relationships, be willing to take part in joint research, design and development activities, and set standards for both the company and for the industry so that the benefits of improved performance will spread."

The new paradigm, then, centers around the words *partnership* and *communications*.

First with MRP II, then with JIT, TQM and CIM, our focus for improvement has been on the factory floor, where labor often accounts for only 10 percent or less of product cost and lead times 20 percent or less of the total.

Yet material cost represents 40, 50 or even as much as 75 percent of the total product cost! It's also the major portion of our inventory investment. And vast amounts of time, people and money go into handling, inspecting, storing and moving purchased materials.

In addition to material cost, supplier lead times are often the major factor limiting our flexibility and hurting our quest for quality. Supplier lead times often represent 80 percent or more of the total amount of time it takes to produce the product, a critical factor in the response time to a customer's need.

And, quite often, about 30 percent of quality problems trace back to purchased material.

"A carefully selected and managed supplier offers the greatest guarantee of consistently high quality," wrote University of San Diego Professor of Marketing and Procurement David N. Burt in the *Harvard Business Review.* "Namely, commitment to the product."

Yet, in many cases, we overlook our suppliers when reaching for World Class performance.

"A World Class company must have World Class suppliers," says Craig Anderson, director of materials at Fisher Controls. "The competition for World Class suppliers will increase as the weak fail. It could really become a seller's market. In fact, the rarest commodity will be World Class suppliers."

Under the old paradigm, we relegated the supplier problems to the Purchasing Department and told them to get us the best price they could...or else. Purchasing's performance measurement was simple— positive variances. That is, if Purchasing could arrange to get materials cheaper, the Purchasing Manager was rewarded. "Negotiate...negotiate" became the exclusive directive. Every penny saved on the invoice price was money in our pocket, so squeeze as much as you can from the supplier's veins. Get several quotes and play one supplier against the other. Suppliers, in fact, are made to be hammered, and if something goes amiss, kick the Purchasing Department a couple of times.

In turn, in order to protect themselves and their suppliers, Purchasing often isolated the suppliers from the rest of the organization with a "no one talks to my supplier" shield.

In the traditional organization, Purchasing came late to the party. Purchasing is often regarded as a clerical function, usually the last to know. Often, neither Purchasing nor the supplier was included in any preliminary or early new product discussions, for example. In the meantime, the pursuit of World Class performance often focused exclusively inside the factory walls.

Purchasing often isolated the suppliers from the rest of the organization.

Getting Off The Floor

Under the old paradigm, people, capital investments and executive time often concentrated on the factory floor. Take a few minutes and list the people and capital in your company being spent on making direct labor more efficient—Industrial Engineers, Manufacturing Engineers, Supervisors, Cost Accountants, Human Resource specialists and the like. Then list the people and money dedicated to working with suppliers—often, the buyer stands alone. Notice the difference in the lengths (and the total amounts) of the two lists. Why the difference? Because, to a great extent, improvements in supplier performance seemed hopeless. "We're just a small duck in a big pond" was the traditional rationale for continuing to live with the status quo and poor supplier performance. Yet, reverse the roles. When a customer comes to us, do we necessarily demand to know whether it's a big customer or a little customer before we deal with them? Of course not! Little customers have a way of becoming big customers.

We tended to view clout as the only hope for improved performance.

Through our old lenses, we tended to view clout—threatening the supplier into submission—as the only hope for improved performance. We needed a "big gun" to hold to our suppliers' heads or they were never going to pay attention.

Yet, the two most glaring examples of using clout—the auto industry and Uncle Sam—are hardly shining examples of World Class performance from suppliers. For example, the wholesale use of clout by the government, insisting on bids, inspections and literally mountains of paperwork for even the most minor of purchases, succeeded in coming up with $500 hammers. Clout failed to deliver, again and again. It didn't even begin to touch on the real root problem, the failure to communicate.

In accordance with our theory on paradigms, we learned to live with the problems, to institutionalize them, to adjust to them. The old paradigm produced painful results—large inventories, erratic demands on our suppliers, long supplier lead times, poor communications, a steady stream of rejects, mountains of "CYA" paperwork, high purchase costs, lack of accountability, incessant finger-pointing, to name a few. In short, our traditional way of dealing with suppliers has lead us to a low quality, high cost, slow response environment...exactly the opposite of what we hope to achieve, World Class performance.

If we want to survive in the global market, if we want to talk in terms of performing to World Class standards, can we really afford to "live with" these problems any more? And if we answer yes, will our customers and competitors answer the same way?

Already, in many industries, the competitive leaders have broken away from the old paradigm to form close partnerships with their suppliers. The results are staggering—supplier lead times cut 50 percent or more, defect-free material delivered 100 percent on time without inspection, frequent delivery of smaller lot sizes without cost penalties and much less paperwork, including purchase orders—some even eliminated invoices and checks.

They did it by creating a new paradigm, by focusing on a number of critical issues:

1) Understanding the difference between purchase cost and purchase price.

2) Putting the correct supplier performance measurements in place.

3) Internal organizational changes, including the creation of supplier teams.

4) Selecting supplier partners based on win-win relationships, not the lowest bid on each specific line item.

The Color Of Money

Let's look at the elements of purchase cost:

1) Invoice price
2) Freight
3) Internal physical activities
    -Inspection

129

-Recounting
-Repackaging
-Store and Issue
4) Paperwork
5) Administration
-Quotes
-Schedule
-Follow-up
6) Scrap, rework or returning defective material

What's the first thing you notice about that list? For a start, these costs are all over the income statement. There's no neat line item for total purchase or acquisition cost. Notice also that the purchase price (the invoice price) is only a part of the purchase cost. Yet traditionally, when we talked about "reducing total purchase cost," weren't we talking almost exclusively about the invoice price? The money we save by reducing paperwork, for example, is the same color as the money we save from cutting the actual invoice price.

Second, those other costs are a significant number—probably a much larger number than you suspect. At Eastman Kodak Copy Products, one of the real success stories in World Class manufacturing, managers were shocked to discover just how large the "hidden" costs of purchased materials were.

"The costs exceeded our wildest dreams," says Dick Psyk of Eastman Kodak. "We were spending three to four times more to plan, procure, ship, receive, inspect, store and dispense material than we believed should be spent. That got a lot of attention."

"We were wasting millions of dollars in line shutdowns due to late deliveries, non-conforming parts—repaired at our expense in many cases—in order to keep the line going," adds William Davis, then Copy Products QA manager.

Notice that a lot of these aspects of purchase *cost* versus purchase *price* are in-house functions, things we can directly attack. They don't require the supplier to do much of anything different. Typically fully 75 percent of our problems with suppliers come from inside our own company. In other words, if 100 percent of our suppliers became perfect tomorrow, we'd still have a problem 75 percent the size of the problem we have today. The excuse that "we can't reduce our *purchase cost* because our suppliers won't cut their *prices*" is a lame one. Much of the opportunity is in our own backyard.

Traditionally, how do we usually attack the question of cost reduction?

The CEO sends a simple memo to Purchasing: "Get the stuff cheaper. In fact, your job performance is going to be judged on how well you do exactly that. Let's take the standard price for a purchased item, then judge how well you're doing by comparing the actual invoice price against the standard. We'll call the measurement Purchase Price Variance, and if you have a positive variance, we'll give you an 'attaboy'. If you have a negative variance, well..."

In the traditional paradigm, the Purchasing Department is like the end of Indiana Jones' bullwhip. When Indy cracks the whip, somewhere out there the end of the whip makes a loud snap. The Purchasing Manager knows his job depends on positive price variances. The first call to "Supplier A" finds that if we buy 1000 components, we get one-half percent price break. If we buy a boatload, we get a two percent break.

Pretty soon the dredges are out building the harbor, and the work is almost completed on the high-rise warehouse, complete with automated inventory retrieval systems to house that boatload of parts.

Did we mention that we only need 100 of those components a year?

The Purchasing Manager quickly realizes that if "Supplier A" will give two percent on a boatload, what will "Supplier B" give? Not to mention "Supplier Z," or "ZZ." So many bids are prepared and sent out to many suppliers. And we know through the industry trade magazine that "Supplier Z" is sweating a little, and we represent a large percentage of "Supplier Z's" business. So maybe we call up and put the squeeze on "Supplier Z's" CEO. Clout that CEO a couple of times on the head for an extra percentage point price break.

Now we've really got those positive variances up there, right?

The Negatives Of Positive Variances

But what else have we done by emphasizing those kinds of practices?

-We've driven inventory costs through the roof.

-We've caused a boom-bust cycle of erratic demand that kills our suppliers.

-In all likelihood, we've guaranteed long lead times, as our suppliers struggle to cope with our erratic demand.

-We've created a huge potential for quality problems, just by large lot sizes alone. In addition, we've hammered our suppliers on price. Is there a potential that our suppliers will cut corners on quality? Of course there is.

Have we kept our costs low?

No, we've actually increased our true costs. We've confused purchase price with purchase costs. The true purchase costs include not only the purchase price, but the costs of quality, paperwork, maintaining inventory, additional transportation costs, additional material handlers, additional Purchasing Department costs for processing multiple quotes and all the other "hidden" costs.

And the lowest bid doesn't necessarily mean the highest quality. Even when quality is high, changing from supplier to supplier not only increases the paperwork load, but puts pressure on Manufacturing because of the "variability" factor. Ask any plant manager—when you get material from three suppliers that meets specs, is it the same? The answer is no. The three lots will run differently. The manufacturing cost will be higher (unfortunately, this is rarely reflected in the purchase cost), and quality will most likely suffer.

Purchase price or purchase cost? Knowing the difference is a vital step on the path to World Class. The key elements to a productive approach include:

The lowest bid doesn't necessarily mean the highest quality.

-Making sure the Quality Specs to the supplier are clear, allowing the supplier to conform without additional inspection.

-Challenging all paperwork and eliminating as much as possible.

-Reducing the number of sources, making it practical for us to uphold our end of the communications requirements.

-Ensuring we have valid, stable schedules and provide our suppliers with visibility of our future needs.

-Making sure the performance measurements encourage and reward all of the above.

Eastman Kodak Copy Products, for example, set up a four-point plan to revamp their dealings with their suppliers:

-Improve the current state of affairs with existing suppliers and existing parts.

-Bring suppliers into the new product design process very early on to prevent new products and new designs of parts from falling victim to the same problems.

-Create a parts certification criteria that would allow Kodak to stop the receiving inspection of material.

-Devise an approach to measuring supplier performance that would provide information for supplier selection, elimination or corrective actions as well as providing feedback to the suppliers on how well their company is performing.

Let's take a closer look at each one of these areas.

Dance With Your Partner

Our first focus, as Eastman Kodak found, is with the suppliers we're already using. Those are, after all, the people who are most likely to become our partners. And they're the people with whom we are more likely to achieve *success*. Part of the fallout of a decade of "Project Team" mentality is a bad case of the all-or-nothing syndrome. In the late 1970s and early 1980s,

133

the push to implement an acronym (usually MRP II at that time) took on the trappings of a holy crusade—with U.S. manufacturing reeling, it's not hard to understand why!

But what we need now are successes—each success we have builds on the previous success. There's a second issue here as well. The low-bid mentality and all its associated ills are so entrenched in American business that the idea of "partnership" can—probably will—involve a major cultural change. One of the most common comments we hear in our Supplier Class goes something like, "We have 50 (or 100 or 1000) suppliers. You can't expect us to be partners with every one of them..."

Of course not.

But how about with one supplier? And if you're successful with that supplier, how about extending the program to another supplier?

Copy Product's Division first step was to identify a team to deal with the suppliers. Because, as we've seen, the issues affecting suppliers cuts across almost all of a company's divisions, that team should reflect all those areas. In Kodak's case, the team included representatives from Product Engineering, the Plant Floor, Purchasing, Materials, Planning and Quality Assurance.

The next step was selecting an established supplier for the program. *Pick the supplier most likely to be successful!* Help your supplier understand your company's vision of the future and how that supplier will fit into that vision. Then build on your successes by adding additional suppliers.

This leads us to one of the touchiest areas of the whole concept of supplier partnerships. The idea of supplier partnerships is based on communications between you and your suppliers. In the real world, *you cannot communicate with thousands of suppliers!* If you work on creating partnerships with your suppliers, it is realistic to expect your supplier base to shrink. Perhaps the most classic example of this is Xerox, who shrank its worldwide supplier base from 5,200 to 356.

The idea of partnership probably will involve a major cultural change.

NUMBER OF SUPPLIERS

BEFORE
AFTER

5000

800

700

750

350

330

196

200

60

107

Pitney
Bowes

Xerox

IBM
(Lexington)

Simon
Telect

Unisys
Plant in N.J.

Too many companies, though, think of Shrinking The Supplier Base as a project in itself. Rather than a *goal*, shrinking the supplier base is a *means to* increase the communications with suppliers necessary to meet the goal. Time that was previously spent on writing and processing competitive bids is spent, instead, on increasing the communications between you and your suppliers.

Simon-Telelect, Inc., a manufacturer of equipment for utility companies, has some impressive improvements in quality and timely performance that directly correlate with supplier base reduction.

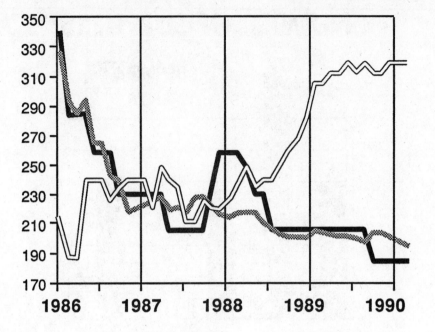

Percent Shipped On Time
_____
=======================

Number of Suppliers
_____
███████████████████████

Percent Rejected
_____
███████████████████████

Reducing the number of suppliers, however, leads to a topic that can throw fear into a purchasing manager's heart—single sourcing. Single sourcing is exactly what the name implies—having just one supplier for a particular material. Traditional thinking, such as that of our Feel Good, Inc. Purchasing Manager, is that single sourcing is giving a supplier a license to steal. And there's a good chance the Purchasing Manager would be looking for another job if caught with only one source, especially if the Purchasing Manager appeared even vaguely friendly with the single source.

Since the company-supplier relationship has been traditionally founded on clout, it only makes sense that when the clout shifts in the other direction, we're going to get clouted—but good!

But is that necessarily true? In a single supplier relationship, might not the supplier be grateful for a long-term, non-bidding commitment? Think of your own situation. If you were approached by a customer who wanted a one-on-one relationship, would you immediately try and gouge them for all they're worth? Of course not. On the flip side, might you be able to concentrate on the idea of partnership more easily with a single supplier than with many? With a single supplier, there's also the fear of getting clobbered by an act of God, the proverbial earthquake that wipes out the single supplier and all the available options, which gives other suppliers the opportunity to do the gouging.

But turn this around. What would your company do if a potential customer came to you in need? You'd roll out the red carpet, showing that you'd make a *great* single source, wouldn't you?

The important thing in considering single sourcing is that it is not an all-or-nothing situation. There may be some items that it makes sense to single source, some that it doesn't. An example of the latter might be a part that is not readily available through other channels without extensive new tooling should the single source be hit by a crippling strike or a fire.

Sharing information, such as material requirements, several weeks beyond the lead time is essential to assist the supplier in doing proper planning. An excellent planning and scheduling system is a common characteristic of most companies that have made major improvements in their purchase costs. Leading by example is another common characteristic. They took their suppliers out on the shop floor and showed them how to reduce lot sizes, put responsibility for quality at the source and how to restructure the supplier's bills of material.

Single sourcing is not an all-or-nothing situation.

Performing To Measure

What we need is a set of supplier performance measurements that evaluates our *total* expectations from our suppliers, not just the purchase price. Let's review a typical set of criteria for evaluating supplier performance:

- -On-time delivery
- -High quality
- -Lead times
- -Price
- -Receiving counts
- -Quick response to information requests
- -Quick feedback of delays

Assign each one of these criteria a value or weight between one and 10, and the total must equal 100. Now give the same list to several people in different departments in your company and ask them to weigh the criteria.

Will anyone's ratings look the same?

Probably not. If the ratings are significantly different, what chance does the supplier have of performing well? Exactly none! Everyone is using different yardsticks.

A large variation in values may also signal significant differences in understanding what's important to us and why. We may have some groups pursuing improvements at the expense of others.

Look at the criteria. Good supplier performance depends not solely on the supplier nor the Purchasing Department. Yet, traditionally, that's where we've placed the burden. Consider that in many companies Purchasing Departments are considered "very protective and defensive." Could they be victims of the environment we created? We think so. Responsibility without control will do that to you!

Partnership is a critical word here.

There's a new joke making the rounds. What, the joke asks, are the three most feared lines in the English language?

"I'm from the corporate office, and I'm here to help you"..."The check is in the mail"...and, "I want to be your partner!"

You cannot order your supplier to be your partner. Detroit tried it, and it was a dismal failure. Clout is out. Partnerships must be earned, the result of both parties deriving benefit from the arrangement. It must be a win-win situation!

And earning a partnership isn't easy. Mutual trust is the foundation of the partnership. That trust requires on-going communications and an open exchange of information that should begin early in the product design phase. But there is no other aspect of manufacturing that can yield such large mutual benefits—we are talking about big dollars here.

One of the first ways we're going to have to change with our suppliers is the way we negotiate. It's hard to expect someone to want to be our partner after we have hammered them into the ground during the negotiations.

"The game of negotiation," wrote Roger Fisher and William Ury in their landmark *Getting To Yes: Negotiating Agreement Without Giving In*, "takes place at two levels. At one level, negotiation addresses the substance; at another, it focuses—usually implicitly— on the procedure for dealing with the substance."

Fisher and Ury suggest four steps to more honest and fair negotiations:

-Separate the people from the problem.

-Focus on interests, not positions.

-Generate a variety of possibilities before deciding what to do.

-Insist that the result be based on some objective standard.

"To sum up," wrote Fisher and Ury, "the principled negotiation method of focusing on basic interests, mutually satisfying options and fair standards typically results in a wise agreement. This method permits you to reach a gradual consensus on a joint decision efficiently without all the transactional costs of digging into positions only to have to dig yourself out of them."

What next? What kind of vision, frontiers, are we looking at? Let's take a peek at that vision:

-Reducing purchase cost 25 percent.
-Reducing lead time on all purchase items to less than four weeks.
-Cutting purchase inventory by 50 percent.
-Reducing the supplier base by two-thirds.

Bringing about these visions is going to be neither fast nor easy—they will require a major change in how we run our businesses.

Let's go back to customer expectations. What does the supplier expect?
1) Clear specifications
2) A fair and reasonable price
3) Stable schedules
4) Visibility of future plans
5) Continued business
6) Respect

Internally, quality specs are going to have to be clear and clearly communicated to our suppliers; delivery schedules will have to be valid and stable—no last-minute fire-fighting. We're going to have to open our doors to our suppliers, open lines of communications—especially in the critical early days of product design. Maybe we need to help our supplier understand our World Class goals. Fisher Controls, for example, has paid the tuition for their suppliers to attend classes on World Class performance.

"You have to develop an education process for both suppliers and the internal organization," says Fisher Control's Craig Anderson. Fisher originally sent all their own buyers to class to gain a better understanding of how a manufacturing company should function in the competitive 1990s. The next step was for the buyers to return to class with the president or vice president from a key supplier, with Fisher picking up the tab. The buyers then continued following up at the suppliers' plants, making sure the communications process was really in place. The emphasis was on, "What can we do for you," not, "What you must do for us to keep our business."

The results have been nothing short of spectacular for both Fisher and its suppliers.

"We've cut our setup times from four to five hours to an hour or two," says Steve Harmon, president of Twin City Die Casting, a Fisher supplier. "We can now economically make smaller runs, matching Fisher's requirements. We now cast only as much as we can machine and immediately machine it. Not only has inventory been reduced by one-third, but quality costs have been reduced by over 50 percent. We've also cut customer lead times by two weeks. The capital freed up by cutting inventory has been put back into better equipment, making us an even better supplier."

For the CEO and executive management, shifting paradigms means focusing on a series of points:

-Make sure supplier and purchasing performance measurements are in line with your expectations.

-Create supplier teams from all departments and empower them to improve supplier performance.

-Develop a policy statement that announces clearly that suppliers are our partners, not our adversaries.

-Develop a policy that defines the conditions where single sourcing is acceptable and where it is not.

-Take visible actions—call your suppliers, go see them, make them feel like partners. Lead by example!

Being a good customer is an essential ingredient to having a good partnership. What does it take to be a good customer?

1) Pay invoices. Having to chase the bucks to get paid after doing a good job is hardly the foundation of a good partnership.

2) Explain why we need to change, to challenge the old paradigms, to become World Class.

3) Make long-term commitments. Commit to be a partner for the long haul. The supplier can then afford

to invest time and capital.

4) Listen to feedback. Communication is a two-way street. There's a lot of brainpower at our disposal, if we choose to listen. Suppliers have a lot of expertise—use their technical talent.

5) Act on suggestions. If we've asked for our suppliers' opinions and then ignore them, what kinds of signals does that send?

6) Provide access to key people. Don't shunt our suppliers off onto side tracks or away from the decision-makers.

7) Avoid finger pointing. When things go wrong—rejects, late deliveries, etc.—focus on getting at the root cause and solving the problem, not on hanging the guilty.

8) Provide visibility of requirements. Constant, last-minute reaction to surprises gets old...and expensive.

9) Stabilize schedules. Delivering on time is tough enough. Hitting a moving target makes it tougher—even impossible.

10) Help with education. We can take a pious position and declare that our suppliers' understanding of the new concepts is the suppliers' problem. In reality, it's a problem for both of us. Share what has worked for us, and why. Encourage and support your suppliers.

"We have to recognize and accept that the customer is the cause of most of the supplier's quality and delivery problems," says Fisher Control's Anderson. "It doesn't make sense for a company to ask its suppliers to do something it isn't doing, and perhaps doesn't even understand."

If we expect to compete in the global market, we must have the cooperation of our suppliers. World Class performance *demands* World Class suppliers. We are not manufacturing islands; instead, we are part of a complicated chain. If our suppliers are our partners instead of our adversaries, then we can focus our total attention on meeting our customers' expectations, which is the key to World Class performance!

1) List current supplier performance criteria and recent performance. Are they properly weighted, agreed upon and not focused on price alone? Are all key criteria measured? Have the results been shared with suppliers? Have you done a root cause analysis and identified the corrective measures needed?

2) Discuss who is responsible for World Class supplier performance.

3) Has the supplier base been reduced to a manageable few?

4) Take the test to determine whether you are a "good customer," then discuss correcting your weak points.

5) Has supplier lead time reduction been a prime target; have lead times been significantly reduced?

6) Identify the true purchase costs.

7) Discuss the current lot sizes and frequency of delivery from suppliers.

8) Discuss the merits of and the concerns about single sources.

9) Discuss the frequency of visits by your key executives to your suppliers.

10) Discuss what benefits your suppliers' technology can bring to your products.

CHAPTER 9

Seeding The Company's Future

Allison was furious, but she was always furious when she was forced to talk to Manufacturing. They were just so smug. "You build the prototype," the Manufacturing foreman, Jesse Roberts, told her, "and we'll figure out a way to manufacture the product, no matter how...painful...the design is." Sure, Manufacturing had to make a few changes, and Allison was more than willing to work the bugs out in ECNs once the line was up and running. That was just the way these things worked. How was she supposed to know all the little problems and nit-picky things that bothered Manufacturing? She was a Design Engineer. The guys in the other building took care of the Manufacturing stuff.

It didn't matter to him that she and three other engineers had been sweating blood for the last eight months over the latest product. And it was a beauty, she thought to herself, smiling. A cutting edge analyzer. She liked that, liked putting together a puzzle where you didn't know the final outcome. Like the tiny little linkage—two solenoids and a handful of gears. Allison had poured over every scrap of literature she could find to come up with the right solenoids. She'd finally found them in France, and had them ship her a dozen. It had taken months, and six of the dozen didn't work. But the ones that did were slick.

Then there was that guy in Purchasing, who had sent her a copy of the company's policies regarding new suppliers. Everybody in the Engineering Department got a kick out of that. How did they expect her and her colleagues to design with all those silly restrictions?

NEW PRODUCT DEVELOPMENT

OLD PARADIGM

- Engineering Job
- Development in Series
- Minimize R&D Costs
- Suppliers Bid After Design
- Create Technical Marvels

NEW PARADIGM

- Company Job
- Concurrent Development
- Develop Products That Sell
- Suppliers Help Design
- Develop What Customers Want

Of course, they were still stinging from the last new product. It had been another cutting edge product, technology that the Research Group had assured them was ages ahead of the nearest competitor. Unfortunately, she thought, the marketplace didn't have sense enough to realize what a good product it was. It had been staying on the shelves in droves.

New products are the lifeblood of a company. New products are even more critical in a World Class economy, because of the increased competitiveness of the market. In other words, if there's a niche, somebody is going to fill it. If that niche happens to be a lower-priced or expanded-features version of one of your mature products, one of your competitors will fill the niche if you don't.

There are other reasons new products have become increasingly necessary for a company to survive.

The global market is more sophisticated than ever. It does, in fact, respond to the idea of "new and improved"—if you don't believe that, you might try talking to the makers of electronic products without remote controls, if you can find any to talk to. Or the makers of eight miles-per-gallon cars, single-flavor soft drinks or one package-design candy bars.

Shifting economic conditions and the new worldwide sensitivity about quality has, we think, created a strong consumer awareness of "value." As we stated earlier, the customer expects value in a product. In many markets, value translates into more or different options, newer technologies, lower prices, greater ease of servicing—all functions of new product development. Remember, we are customer-driven. We respond to our market. New products are the heart and soul of that response.

And, as markets become more niche-oriented, the first person into the niche enjoys a tremendous advantage.

Second, we are in business to turn a profit. Our ability to minimize product cost is inherent in the development stage! The decisions we make in the design stage will determine as much as 80 percent of the cost of the product. Nowhere is this clearer than in the automobile industry. In the frantic search to discover why Japanese cars were less expensive to manufacture than American cars, the difference came down again and again to product design. According to McKinsey & Co., for example, American car doors cost twice as much as the equivalent Japanese car door, and 75 percent of that difference was rooted in the product's design.

That's what we mean when we talk about the concept of designing for manufacturability. While a mature product might still have a significant market share, our thoughts of continuous improvement also apply to the bottom line. If we can create a product that is both less expensive and easier to manufacture, we'll meet both our customers' raised expectations and simultaneously improve our bottom line.

A mature product line might not be able to take advantage of newer, more efficient processes, equipment or techniques that could result in increased profit margins or quality improvements. In the electronics industry, for example, an older product might not be able to take advantage of surface mount technology, which allows components to be placed closer together on the printed circuit board than the older hand-placement allowed. Surface mounting allowed a manufacturer to take advantage of an automated process; it also allowed product to be made smaller, thanks to tighter "packing." The smaller packages hit a nerve with consumers, who suddenly realized they were sick of big boxes sitting on their desks.

In other words, the first users of surface mount technology were able to raise the expectations of their customers in regard to small size, and then meet those raised expectations. Companies that had never considered the size of the box important found themselves playing catch-up in a race to be small.

Instead of concentrating on the cutting edge of technology, the emphasis is instead on technology transfer, the ability to get useable technology to market.

Cutting development time and cost for new products is, in fact, becoming the new rallying cry for American business, much as such acronyms as MRP II, JIT and CIM have been in the past. The new acronym is CE, for concurrent engineering. The best definition of concurrent engineering is Japanese, and it boils down to designing the product and the process to manufacture the product at the same time. In actuality, though, those words aren't broad enough. New product development encompasses more than engineering know-how. It cuts completely across the company, from Research through Finance, touching on production planning, suppliers, order entry, field service and more.

New product development, then, should be an activity that draws resources from every part of the company, concurrent development rather than concurrent engineering.

Let's think first about our existing paradigm for new product development.

PRODUCT DEVELOPMENT

• OLD PARADIGM: Relay Race •

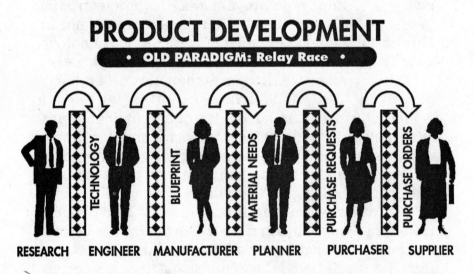

| RESEARCH | ENGINEER | MANUFACTURER | PLANNER | PURCHASER | SUPPLIER |

For a start, imagine a fortress surrounded by a series of walls. At the center of the fortress, wearing heavy armor and riding chargers, are the Engineers. They are at the center of the fortress because they are the Creators, the Wizards who create new products. And they're very, very good at creating new products.

They know the latest bells and whistles. They read all the technical journals. And they have help from Wizards in Research, who are constantly casting the bones looking for the newest, the most untested, technologies. Once the Research Wizards craft the technologies, they whisper in the Engineers' ears, and the process gets under way.

The Engineers lovingly craft the new product, dealing directly with suppliers, blending and mixing and building until they have the Product—at least, on paper.

Then, with appropriate ceremony, the Engineers throw the specs and drawings and bill of material over the wall to Manufacturing, who are sort of in the position of Royal Retainers. They take the documentation for the new product, puzzle over it, and try to figure out how they can manufacture it. The Manufacturing Retainers may puzzle over the fact that there are 25 different thread sizes for screws or that the main ingredient for the next blend won't correctly meter in the company's machines, but the ways of the Knights of Engineering aren't necessarily understood by mortal men. After an appropriate period of fretting and purification, Manufacturing lobs the documentation to Planning. Planning is like Ladies in Waiting, although there's some question as to what they're waiting for. As soon as they have the documentation, they pour over their own arcane documents, master schedules and the like, shake their heads, then lob the whole mess over the wall to Purchasing, who must figure out what the Engineers really want. As Exchequers for the Castle, Purchasing is charged with getting supplies as cheaply as possible. Purchasing also doesn't understand why Engineering specified the main component as they did, since that means the component can only be obtained from one supplier, who works out of a tent east of the Dutchy of Cleveland. But, after the extra sweating, fretting and bidding, the now-battered paperwork is hurled over the wall to Accounting, which scratches in the sand trying to figure out what the thing really costs. Someone eventually throws the paperwork to the Suppliers, who are little more than Barbarians

149

At The Gate. The Suppliers scratch themselves through their untanned animal skins, agree that of course they can meet the delivery requirements, take the contract and ride off across the tundra, only to be heard from much, much later. Eventually the material trickles in, and Manufacturing actually builds the product, then tosses the thing to Sales and Marketing, often referred to as the Court Jesters, who try to figure out if there are any customers who actually want to buy it.

And so on and so on, until one afternoon, someone on the loading dock hurls the finished product over the last retaining wall to the customers, who, more often than not, are puzzled at why they couldn't have had the same product two years earlier, 20 percent cheaper and in red.

And we get clobbered.

All too frequently, Sales and Marketing is questioning the abilities of Engineering, Engineering is looking down on Manufacturing, and Manufacturing is using everyone's name in vain as it struggles with the new product. Research and Development is pushing new technologies, and executive management is tightening the thumbscrews on deadlines. Daniel E. Whitney of Charles Stark Draper Laboratory, Inc., described it this way: "...Design has become a bureaucratic tangle, a process confounded by fragmentation, overspecialization, power struggles and delays..."

We've already looked at a few of the stakes in the marketplace, but there's an opportunity in bottom-line terms as well. In modern high-tech industries, research and development costs are often as significant as labor and overhead costs combined. Under the old paradigm, we knew we were doing well if we allocated a certain percentage of our income to Research and Development, essentially throwing money at the problem. Under the new paradigm, the issue is the productivity of that investment, measured by the percentage of our sales derived from new products. If the new products don't sell, it doesn't matter how much money we're pouring into Research and Development—it's not working.

> **Research and development costs are often as significant as labor and overhead costs combined.**

What kind of numbers are we talking about here? Hewlett-Packard, one of the most successful American companies in terms of new product development, derives more than 50 percent of sales from products developed within the last three years!

We have to remember that the reason we allocate large dollars to Research and Development is not to prove the manhood of the Engineering Department, be on the cutting edge of either technology or automation, or even to test our ability to manage costs within the budget. The intent is to turn out products that customers buy, and we make a profit. If we're spending a lot and making a lot, that's good. If we're spending a lot and not selling a lot, it doesn't matter whether Engineering is under budget or not. According to one oft-cited study by McKinsey & Co., going 50 percent over budget during development to get a new product out on time or sooner reduces total profit by only four percent. Staying on budget and getting to market six months late reduces profits by 33.3 percent!

Even if your Research and Development costs are on target, there's still the opportunity to increase your efficiency and leverage your Research and Development dollar by reducing the "re's:"
-Re-designing the product
-Re-doing the drawings
-Re-placing the documentation
-Re-structuring bills of material
-Re-purchasing materials
-Re-working materials to the latest revision

According to the Commerce Department's National Institute of Standards and Technology, the payoffs for designing for manufacturability, quality and ease of maintenance are tremendous:
-Development time, 30-70 percent less
-Engineering changes, 65-90 percent fewer
-Time-to-market, 20-90 percent less
-Overall quality, 200-600 times higher
-White-collar productivity, 20-110 percent higher
-Dollar sales, 5-50 percent higher
-Return-on-assets, 20-120 percent higher

Intermec Corp. uses an interesting statistic, based on work done by MIT's Leaders for Manufacturing program: During the first 15 percent of a new product development cycle, we make decisions that affect 85 percent of a product's cost and quality.

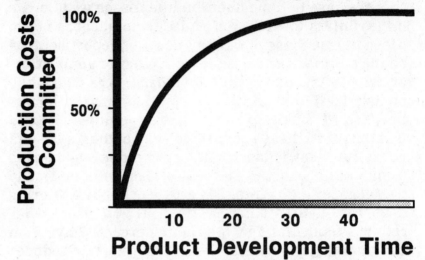

A corollary to that observation is that the further along a product gets in development, the harder it is to make changes that don't engender huge costs. It's easy to make changes in a product's case size while it's still on the proverbial drawing board; a lot harder when we've invested $10 million in a plastic casting machine to build the case. According to the research firm DataQuest, Inc., a major change in an electronic product that would cost $1,000 during the design phase would cost $10,000 during design testing, $100,000 during process planning, $1,000,000 during test production and as high as $10,000,000 during final production!

Process, Not Product

According to MIT's *Made In America*, "U.S. firms are still devoting only a third of their research expenditures to the improvement of process technology; the other two-thirds is allocated to the development of new and improved products. In Japan, these proportions are reversed."

To summarize, in the old paradigm, new product development is the exclusive province of the Engineering—or the Research and Development—portion of the company. New product development takes place in a series—one department finishes, then passes the product onto the next department. New product development is closely held, done entirely inside the company. We'll let our suppliers know what we want from them when we're about ready to go. Finally, we are fascinated with over-engineering or adding-to—the ideal product is 100 percent computerized and has tail fins. The results are numerous conflicts, a long development time, lots of revisions at every stage and high product development cost.

The conflicts and inefficiencies in the new product development process occur because:

1) People don't understand the benefits of cooperation.

2) People haven't been coached on the proper methods, tools and techniques to get that cooperation.

3) Personal or departmental goals get put before company objectives.

4) Bad methods or procedures waste time and resources, causing inadequate time to consider other departments' requirements.

5) The focus is placed on departmental or individual self-serving goals rather than on the expectations of the customer and the company.

The result is that the creation of new products is like starting to paint your house before you have firmly decided what colors to use. The result of the many changes is cost overruns, schedule overruns and a painter who isn't happy with anyone at all. If too many changes are made, chances are the quality is poor and no one is happy.

How should the new paradigm look?

1) New product development is different from new product design. New product design is only one phase, the Engineering phase. New product development is a company-wide activity, with all areas of the company participating from the beginning. It includes the design of the product, the process to manufacture the product,

New product design is only one phase.

the sales and marketing strategy for the new product—every aspect of the product.

2) The first step comes from an awareness of the customers' expectations—what can we do to raise those expectations?

3) We are critically concerned with designing for manufacturability, which includes the three elements of our Mission Statement—high-quality, low-cost and flexibility.

4) We concurrently develop the new product. We develop the process for manufacturing the new product at the same time we develop the product itself. Plant floor people who will make the product participate as co-equals with design engineers.

5) Our major suppliers are involved from the beginning. We make use of their technical expertise and knowledge to smooth our development process.

The new paradigm allows the product development activities to occur concurrently, not as the sole effort of one particular group.

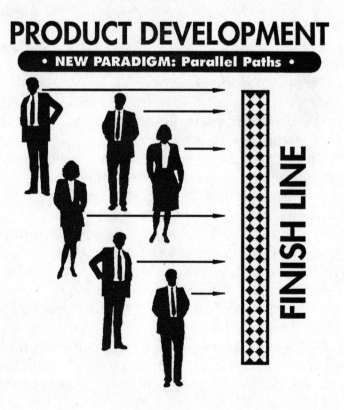

PRODUCT DEVELOPMENT
• NEW PARADIGM: Parallel Paths •

FINISH LINE

A Company Effort

Product development is a company job.

"Product development is just one of the steps in manufacturing a successful product," says Joe Beebe of Intermec. "It just happens to be the first step."

Bently Nevada uses an excellent process that breaks new product development into four steps:

1) Identify Market Needs
2) Define The Products To Be Developed
3) Design The Products
4) Introduce The Products

Identify Market Needs centers around discovering what the customers really want. Under the old paradigm, needs were viewed drastically differently, more knee-jerk or reactive, less concerned with the impact of the development on our total resources. We often chased customer orders. A salesman went out, came back with an order and we developed what was basically a new product. We didn't assess the real market need. We didn't go through any formal process. If the customer wanted it in pink, then we made one in pink. Other times, we reacted to a "hot" new technological breakthrough, pressure from another department, cost-cutting directives or management pushes for something new. It's analogous to the informal systems that grow up on the plant floor in the absence of a formal system. People and equipment became less effective, reducing capacity, as the operator hopped from one "hot job" to the next. We shipped the product, even if it cost us a fortune. We will develop new products, but the impact on Engineering will be the same as on the plant floor. The challenge under the new paradigm is to manage the development of those new products. Just like on the shop floor, we have resource constraints—Research and Engineering time, Manufacturing capabilities, Management goals and strategies, Financial objectives, and others—and we have to make the best choices within those constraints.

Under the old paradigm, Management often issued edicts on when the new product was due and how

We often chased customer orders.

155

much we could spend to develop it, or Research and Development came up with some technological breakthrough. Everyone else scrambled to design and develop the products. Demonstrated capacity in Engineering is reduced and costs go up.

In the new paradigm, though, this phase becomes much less parochial and better thought out. We begin by answering some basic questions. How do we determine what the customer wants? What are the real expectations? What are the risks and rewards of new technology? What is the impact on existing resources if we proceed?

The question of customer expectations is the beginning.

Everyone else scrambled to design and develop the products.

"You can't just step out and ask the customer what they want," says Dave Biggs of Bently Nevada. "Instead, you ask what problems they're having, and what might best solve those problems."

At Bently Nevada, the first step is a Proposal Review Board (PRB) that includes the heads of all functional departments and is chaired by the company president—basically the same group involved in the SOP process. Intermec uses an Executive Review Board that serves the same purpose.

The function of these boards is to review all the "wants" from customers, from Sales and Marketing, from Engineering, from Research, from Executive Management and then decide upon which projects to allocate the limited resources to develop. Everyone has different ideas on which products the company should proceed with. Sales and Marketing wants more options; Manufacturing wants products suited to the equipment they have and that is easy to produce; Research has a couple of new technological wrinkles they'd love to get to the marketplace; Finance has cost-cutting goals; Executive Management has a strategic direction for the company. All these areas have "candidates" for new products. We can't make them all. No one has unlimited resources. The purpose of that first step is to hash through all the options, bring the conflicts out into the open, and resolve those conflicts. The objective is to decide the best use of the resources for the company and the customer.

The recurring theme here is communications. Sales and Marketing has its needs lists. There's a wealth of information in customer complaints and the Service Department. People in the field are good sources of input. All the companies mentioned in this book have also made great strides in introducing the people who design and make the product to the people who buy the product. It can be a planned program like Trane's, where production technicians are sent on location, to where the commercial air conditioners are being installed. Or it can be planned meetings between team members and customers, all aimed at tracking down those elusive expectations. Fisher Controls, for example, has a regular program for taking plant floor people, purchasing, and others out to meet with customers, aimed at getting to the real customer expectations.

There are two other areas of input in the *Identifying Market Needs* stage: Technology and Management. Technology is a two-edged sword. Because we have (or think we can develop) the technology, we have a tendency to use it. In some cases, we have a mandate to use it.

It goes back to the American fascination with technology, and the sense that the most technologically successful product will triumph in the marketplace—not necessarily the case.

"The way to make progress," says Dale Esse of Kodak Copy Products, "is to manage technological innovation."

Accordingly, Copy Products tries to hold technological innovations to a reasonable number in new products.

"At times, we want to hit singles," says Esse. "Not home runs."

The "singles" vs. "home runs" analogy is a critical point in new product development. Singles might best be defined as incremental improvements in existing product lines, or evolutionary changes in products. The home run, on the other hand, is exactly the paradigm-shifting product that vaults its makers ahead of the competition.

The singles vs. home runs analogy is a critical point.

"If there's a fundamental paradigm shift going on in your industry, you've got no choice but to go for a home run," says Dave Biggs. "But the street is littered with people who tried to muscle a home run."

Probably the most spectacular body is the corpse of General Electric's rotary compressor for refrigerators. GE staked it's entire $2 billion refrigerator business on the new compressor design, the result of a crash research program using untested technology in the mid-1980s.

Despite worries from lower level technicians, none of the problems was communicated up through the six-level chain of command. Testing was "accelerated," and keeping to the schedule was paramount. GE built a $120-million automated factory to build the new compressors, eventually cranking out more than one million refrigerators before the first compressor failed. Before it was over, GE had replaced 1.1 million defective compressors and taken a $450-million pretax charge in 1988. The factory was shifted over to manufacturing air conditioner compressors on contract for Fedders Corp. Swinging the bat for home runs can be expensive.

If he had it to do over, GE's Chief of Technology and Manufacturing Richard Burke told *The Wall Street Journal*, "I'd have gone and found the lowest damn level people we had...and just sat down in their little cubbyholes and asked them, 'How are things today?'"

The balance between the singles and the home runs is critical. Hewlett-Packard, for example, maintains a careful balance between their long-term research and their short-term applied R&D. Frank Carrubba, director of H-P's labs, describes their central lab as, "R&D with a capital 'R' and small 'd,' while divisions do R&D with a small 'r' and a capital 'D.'"

Define The Products

The second phase of Bently Nevada's product development cycle is *defining the products* to be developed. A product development team is assembled, which should include representatives from Engineer-

---

Intermec also encouraged shop floor input.

---

ing, Manufacturing, the shop floor, Marketing, Cost Accounting, Purchasing and our major suppliers. At Intermec, new product development falls under a program manager, who, in turn, draws his or her team from all areas of the company. The team is empowered to make critical decisions without getting bogged down by bureaucratic red tape. Authority is spread out among the ranks. The objective is, early on, to bring in experts from all areas of the company.

"Communications is the biggest challenge here," says Biggs.

A good example of the success of the team approach is the creation of Intermec's newest printer for bar code labels. It doesn't look like other bar code printers—usually square boxes. Instead, it's small and rounded—because one of the questions the team asked was whether "square" was the most efficient shape for a printer that used round rolls of paper. Intermec also encouraged shop floor input, which resulted in a printer that snapped together, requiring fewer tools to put it together. It has also resulted in a shop floor that's enthusiastic about the new machine. When the first printers rolled off the line, the whole factory stopped for a major party.

"Everybody," notes Biggs of Bently Nevada, "likes to be part of a win."

The printer was also brought to the market in a quarter of the time previously spent on new product development, which gave Intermec Corp. an edge in an increasingly competitive market.

At the product definition step, we're turning wishes into specifications, and, again, there are going to be conflicts.

"There's nothing wrong with conflict," says Biggs. "Say we're trying to build the best car we can. Engineering automatically thinks heads-up display like an F-16; Sales wants sports car performance; Finance wants 250 miles per gallon and a list price of $1,500. Manufacturing wants them suited for mass production, not specials. We have to have a way to resolve those conflicts."

One of the ways those conflicts gets resolved is to

159

get each party to explain their needs in users' terms. Customer expectations is again the key.

Expectations are tricky, at best. Often, the question of expectations falls into subjective areas. Take, for example, Mazda's spectacular introduction of the Miata ragtop sports car. The Miata was designed to fill a certain very specific niche—sports car enthusiasts who fondly remembered, or had read about, the old days of Porsche 356 "bathtubs" and MG open sports cars. To be sure, the customer expected a certain level of performance and styling, but beyond that, Mazda product developers had to ferret out other, less obvious expectations. Such as how the exhaust should sound; the feel of the gearshift lever; even the relationship between the seat and the window to allow the driver and passenger to ride with their elbows out.

Had Mazda simply put together a focus group of customers and asked them questions, it's unlikely that the sound of the exhaust system would have ever come up.

The result of all Mazda's homework is one of the most successful new car introductions of the decade.

Another tool Bently Nevada uses in the *Definition* phase is the "Fast Prototype." The idea is to get out a real-life example ASAP for people to examine, touch, etc.

"The best way to communicate how something is going to look and feel is to build one," Biggs says. "In five minutes with a dummy product, I'll communicate more than I ever will on 8 1/2 X 11-inch sheets of paper filled with words."

The Fast Prototype stage allows Bently Nevada to head off design problems that would not normally have surfaced until much later, when the words had been turned into something tangible, thus heading off expensive redesign.

Other actions happen in this phase, including costing, revenue estimates and the like.

The Fast Prototype stage allows Bently Nevada to head off design problems.

Design The Product

Product Design moves us into the realm of designing for manufacturability, with the team looking at such issues as quality, manufacturability, user friendliness and serviceability.

During this phase, we need to address the basic issues of the process, which we are designing parallel with the product. We need to answer questions about production planning, customer lead time versus manufacturing lead time and other issues. These points are critical to the manufacturing process—if customer lead time is one week, for example, and manufacturing lead time is 20 weeks, we're vulnerable to forecast error, especially if we're dealing with many products or options. The problem can be softened if we carry lots of inventory to protect against high variations versus the plan, but that's an expensive solution. Sales needs to be in on this discussion to understand early the implications of process and product design on forecasting. Purchasing and suppliers need to be involved at this stage to assess capacity requirements and real costs. "The price a supplier gives the Engineer isn't always the price they give Purchasing," according to Dave Biggs.

We also begin to address such issues as documentation—what documentation does Manufacturing need to make the product? Creating drawings in Engineering of items Manufacturing never plans to make or adding levels to bills of material that aren't needed can be very expensive, non-value-adding activities. Are we going to keep inventory in finished goods or raw materials? Is order entry done by end item or SKU numbers? These issues should be addressed during—not after—design. The more we do in parallel, the shorter the time to market.

"We want to do as much in parallel as possible," Biggs says. "The pros are that the project gets done quickly and the right attributes get designed in. The cons are that changes in the design have broad impact. The key to successful paralleling is a good, detailed execution plan."

We want to do as much in parallel as possible.

"The more parallel you run," says Bob Kuehn, director of Product Assurance at Intermec, "the more weaknesses in the process you reveal while you still have time to correct them."

Being Introduced

In this phase, the product is getting ready to go into full manufacture. There are, according to Bently Nevada, a series of steps:
    -Answer questions quickly and accurately
    -Correct defects immediately
    -Keep track of enhancement requests
    -Prioritize and execute the appropriate enhancements
    -Keep the company at large informed of the status of the project.

"A key principle here is that process development needs to be as effectively managed as product development," Biggs says.

What's the quality of both the product and process development? Quality can be measured. The expectations were that products would be produced that customers would buy, didn't have to be re-designed and were profitable. Actual sales compared to plan, volume of engineering changes in the first year and actual costs are valid quality measurements.

New products need to be included in the SOP process as soon as possible, before the first production run. Otherwise, capacity planning can suffer, plus, there's no effective way to phase out the old product while phasing in the new.

From The Ground Up

There are obstacles to the new paradigm, among them the mindsets of the various departments. In a less competitive market, Engineering may have had the time to constantly refine a new product before we launched it. In an overheated global market, time-to-market becomes the make-or-break factor. Performance to schedule in engineering becomes every bit as critical as performance to schedule on the plant floor.

"We believe the single most important factor in determining a product's profitability is time to market," says Biggs. "In the search for time, that means you design for your strengths. If Manufacturing says this is the process they do best, we have to think a long time before we let Engineering not use that process."

Engineering itself may be under the gun timewise. We have actually heard the words, "When you're not busy with your regular work, why don't you whip up some new product ideas?" Who, exactly, is not busy with their regular work?

Manufacturing may be accustomed to offering off-the-cuff suggestions without any real knowledge of the product design process. Or they may not know the way to communicate their ideas to Engineering. For too long we've allowed, even encouraged, an adversarial relationship between our departments.

We may have too much inventory of the old product to quickly release the new product. There's a line that all of us who've ever been involved with new product development have heard, and that line goes something like, "Can you stall it for a few months until we empty out the warehouse of last year's model..."

And maybe the rest of the company feels uncomfortable becoming involved in the new product development program. Maybe they've put in their ideas before, only to have them snubbed. Maybe they don't know the best way to communicate their ideas.

In our classes, we've accumulated a list of new product development time and cost obstacles that's worth sharing:

-Creeping elegance

-Undefined market need

-Technical "surprises"

-Underfunding

-Shifting priorities of engineering efforts

-Bill of material, drawings, specs and documentation inaccuracies

-Late deliveries of material for prototype and initial production

-Time and costs to scrap and rework

-Untrained work force
-Tooling not available
-Lack of manufacturing capacity

The answer to these problems and obstacles lies in adopting the new paradigm, with its focus on meeting customer expectations, parallel development and company-wide involvement.

Intermec has also added another step to its product development cycle that has paid off handsomely. The Quality Lab is basically a shop floor laboratory that helps the new product development team refine the young product. The first step requires the engineer to precisely define what the product is supposed to do. You would be surprised at the number of problems this step alone heads off.

At selected stages in the development, the prototype is sent to the lab for independent testing. The results, then, are quickly available, and necessary changes can be incorporated at a much earlier stage.

What are the payoffs of successful product development?

At Bently Nevada, a design challenge was to create an instrument to supersede a mature—and very successful—product. The team effort resulted in a product, the 3300, that has fewer parts, takes fewer tools to manufacture, costs 20 percent less than the original product and still makes an excellent profit.

One of the most striking examples of designing for manufacturability comes when watching the assembly of the old case versus the assembly of the new case. The old case has literally hundreds of parts, requiring dozens of different tools and careful alignment for assembly. The new case has one-third the parts and mostly snaps together, requiring a screwdriver and a wrench for assembly.

In its circuit board design, Bently Nevada made the interesting decision to add some parts that had been options on the previous model. Why would they choose to add parts? For a start, the new model could be changed in the field, a plus for the customer. The parts added—resistors and capacitors—were cheap,

The answer lies in adopting the new paradigm.

non-heat-producing, and had minimal effects on the unit cost and on operating specs. And by eliminating an option by making it a standard feature, Bently Nevada was able to make major gains in manufacturing— eliminating a level in the bill of material, eliminating forecasting and scheduling problems and, by reducing a manufacturing step, reducing the manufacturing lead time.

The 3300, by the way, took one-third the time to develop as previous Bently Nevada products.

Who Expects What?

One of the biggest flaws in our old paradigm has been that the customers were at the end of the "food chain." We designed products from the inside-out; that is, we started with Engineering and ended up with the customers. The result is that we all too often designed a great product that nobody wanted, took too long to do it and spent too much money in the process.

Of course, the all-time classic example is Ford's introduction of the Edsel in the 1950s. The Edsel was an excellent car for the times, an engineering tour de force. It was also overpriced and dreadfully ugly. Now the only thing that remains of the Edsel is its name, which is synonymous with "white elephant."

The second question is, "What can we do to raise our customers' expectations, then meet those rising expectations?"

The theme of raised expectations is part of being a World Class manufacturer. Customers' expectations change rapidly and, more often than not, those changes represent raised expectations. Just a few years back, no one even thought of asking for a remote control device for their television set. Now, the same market wouldn't think of buying a television set without one.

If you have the flexibility that comes with World Class performance standards, you are in a position to respond to technological innovations that result in raised customer expectations.

In high tech industries such as personal computers, we already see flexibility—that is, short time to

The 3300 took one-third the time to develop as previous products.

market, quick response to market and product mix shifts, the ability to customize and meet the customers' expectations—becoming one of the key competitive issues. It is not a question of who can get the fastest personal computer to the marketplace first, but rather who can match the machine to the market's continually rising expectations.

The more competitive a marketplace, the bigger the premium for effectively and quickly transferring technology into products that both meet customer expectations and can be produced profitably—the seeds of a company's future.

DISCUSSION POINTS

1) How are the conflicts between needs for new products as seen by Sales, Marketing, Engineering, Research and Manufacturing considered and resolved?

2) Discuss how customer needs are currently determined and decisions made to allocate development resources. Discuss strengths, weaknesses and problems with the current process.

3) Discuss the parallel vs. series or concurrent approach to product development. Which approach best describes your company?

4) Discuss the "home run vs. singles" strategy for developing products and processes. Which best suits your company?

5) Are product specifications put into easily "visualized" terms and tested for customer reaction prior to Engineering starting to design?

6) Are Engineering priorities constantly shifting?

7) When are the following issues considered and defined for new products?
   - a) Expected customer delivery lead time
   - b) Anticipated Manufacturing lead time (including Purchasing)
   - c) Forecasting detail required
   - d) What stage or level to keep inventory and how much
   - e) Production cost
   - f) Order entry method
   - g) Documentation requirements from Engineering for the suppliers and plant floor
   - h) Manufacturing methods or processes

8) What percentage of this year's sales is derived from products introduced over the last two to three years? Is the number satisfactory? If not, what is the goal?

9) How many Engineering changes are occurring in the first year after a new product is released?

10) What is the current length of time it takes to develop new products?

Measuring to Perform

Roberts was despondent. After six months of R&D and two more months of feasibility, his pet project, a revision of one of the production lines, was about to end up on the financial scrap-heap.

What was worse was that Finance was so sympathetic.

It was a good project, they agreed, but there was just no way to bring it off at a reasonable cost. The problem, Finance told Roberts, was overhead cost.

The new line, Finance said, was just too overhead-intensive.

Plus, Diane Dill from Finance continued, there was the question of new equipment. The new line would require a substantial capital investment, and no matter how she massaged the numbers, the return-on-investment looked bad.

Roberts had argued—it was, after all, his baby—the new machinery would allow a more fluid process-type line, not to mention help solve the quality problems that had been haunting the products produced on that line. They would be more flexible, because changeover time would be negligible and the lead time would be reduced to only a few minutes.

Look at more than just the numbers, Roberts begged, but the woman just shook her head.

We're a public company, she had said. Every three months we have to justify ourselves to our board of directors and our stockholders.

Feel Good had done a great job of tracking direct labor—in fact, they had it down to a fraction of a penny—three-decimal-place precision. Overhead costs were allocated based on direct labor, and while Roberts'

PERFORMANCE MEASUREMENTS

OLD PARADIGM

- Measure What's Easy
- Measure Utilization & Efficiency
- Allocate Overhead by Direct Labor
- Focus on Direct Labor
- Justify by ROI

NEW PARADIGM

- Measure What's Important
- Measure Total Quality
- Allocate Overhead by Meaningful Activ.
- Elim. Unnecessary $
- Jusitfy to Improve Flexibility

---

idea had merit, the direct labor hadn't been reduced very much; thus overhead costs were "apparently" excessive.

Focusing on direct labor had allowed the company to really drive down direct labor cost, which implied reductions in the allocated overhead. Although, Roberts thought wryly, it didn't seem that overhead had really been driven down. What had really been driven down was employee morale on the shop floor, where they seemed to be trying to do more in less time. Well, he guessed it was all good for the bottom line.

The bottom line, was, after all, the bottom line.

The bottom line.
Ultimately, that's the scorecard on which a manufacturing business—any business—is judged.

Yet we are learning, slowly and with no small amount of pain, that knowing the bottom line is not always enough.

Like our manufacturing processes themselves, our performance measurement and cost accounting systems evolved slowly over the years out of certain basic assumptions. Those assumptions grew from the traditional paradigms, solid as rocks, as solid as a black bottom line.

As our manufacturing processes have changed drastically in the last 10 years, performance measurements and accounting practices simply have not kept pace.

"Manufacturing performance measures that lack congruence with the competitive thrusts of business may become the corporate millstones of the 1990s," reported the Boston University School of Management Manufacturing Roundtable in 1987. "Manufacturing performance measures, as currently articulated, may be the greatest impediments to continued progress."

In fact, the entire panoply of measurement systems and cost accounting systems is seriously flawed. Robert S. Kaplan, professor and co-author of *Relevance Lost: The Rise And Fall Of Management Accounting*, puts it bluntly:

"Companies who are trying to become globally

competitive will find it hard to do so with a traditional accounting (and measurement) system(s)."

There are basically four overlapping and, to a large extent, interdependent areas in the performance measurement/cost accounting question:

1) Performance measurements to monitor the quality of our business management process.

2) Accounting issues to satisfy external reporting requirements and internal cost management objectives.

3) Product costing for strategic decisions.

4) Justification for capital expenditures.

"In the future," says Dan Owens, director of finance at Fisher Controls, "we must differentiate between the measurements necessary for operation performance, external reporting and business planning."

Because the areas overlap, it's not unusual for some experts to lump them all in the single category of "cost accounting" or "manufacturing accounting." The problems in all four areas were neatly summed up by the Computer Aided Manufacturing International (CAM-I) coalition when they put together their CAM-I Conceptual Design for manufacturing accounting.

"Existing cost accounting systems and cost management practices cannot serve the objectives of automated manufacturing environments because they:

"Do not adequately trace costs.

"Do not isolate the costs of unnecessary activities.

"Do not penalize overproduction.

"Do not adequately quantify the importance of non-financial measures such as quality, throughput and flexibility.

"Do not support the justification of new investments in advanced manufacturing technology, and fail to monitor the benefits obtained."

In other words, the old paradigm is badly in need of an overhaul. Let's see if we can isolate the basic assumptions the current manufacturing accounting and performance measurement paradigms rest on:

1) Measure what's easiest to measure. If we can measure it, we must need the figures for something. (Sounds suspiciously like the old Howard Ruff saw of,

Companies. . . trying to become globally competitive will find it hard to do so with a traditional accounting system(s).

"When you've got a hammer, everything looks like a nail," doesn't it?).

2) Focus on sub-optimization. We never saw the process as a whole, only the pieces. We isolated activities on separate islands, then launched a myopic effort to maximize the performance of that particular island, without regard to the impact on the other islands or the organization as a whole—the Engineering budget or Manufacturing Department efficiency, for example.

3) Use some performance measurements as motivators by setting goals or quotas artificially low to ensure that people could or would exceed them. Sales quotas and time standards are good examples.

4) Allocate overhead by direct labor. Every direct labor dollar spent represents a multiplier of the overhead expenses spent—often as much as $10 of overhead for every $1 of direct labor.

5) Based on number four, reductions in direct labor costs will result in large reductions of overhead costs.

6) Over-absorbing overhead produces more profit for the company.

7) Track direct labor as closely as possible, because that's the way we chip away at inefficiencies in our manufacturing processes. It's also the way we keep tabs on our workers.

8) Make as much as possible, spread the fixed cost over more units and maximize profit.

9) Justify capital expenditures through traditional return-on-investment (ROI) analysis.

The Heisenberg Uncertainty Principle

"During the first part of this century, cost accounting was developed primarily to meet the requirements of product costing data and inventory valuation for external reporting purposes," says Owens of Fisher Controls. "The measurement and accounting systems focused on mass production and direct labor. During the next 40-50 years, operating management determined the need to measure performance on the

We launched a myopic effort to maximize the performance of each particular island. . .

factory floor, and since the only readily available data was provided by cost accounting, that's what formed the basis for today's systems."

Using cost accounting data for performance measurements was basically what the military likes to call a "field expedient solution." We needed some way to measure our then-new process—mass production. Our Finance Department had already assembled a vast amount of data for the IRS, the SEC and other external organizations. So we piggybacked one on the other. Our methods of measuring performance, then, like our accounting systems, grew up when direct labor amounted to a much larger proportion of the total cost of a product. Second, from Finance's viewpoint, direct labor was easier to track than more amorphous expenses like overhead. Not surprisingly, our performance measurement systems tend to be geared toward measuring the performance of direct labor:
-Direct labor utilization
-Direct labor efficiency
-Machine utilization

We needed some way to measure our new process— mass production.

In the early part of the century, German physicist Werner Heisenberg noted strange behavior among atoms he was observing. To describe the action of the atoms, he formulated the Heisenberg Uncertainty Principle, which, loosely stated, says that the very act of observing anything changes that which is observed. Regardless of whether it's true for atoms, the Uncertainty Principle holds true on the factory floor. It's not what you expect, but what you inspect that counts. If you measure the number of pieces a worker produces, and the worker knows that the more pieces produced, the better the worker looks, guess what happens? Right—lots of pieces produced.

Look at how these performance measures have affected the way we run our businesses:
-An emphasis on performance to time standards tends to place priority on working on the "easy" jobs, perhaps at the expense of quality or customer service.
-Too much attention to direct labor, which, remember, often represents 15 percent or less of the

total product cost, can be diverting attention away from larger cost elements that should be managed more closely.

-Focusing on machine utilization tends to result in excess inventory, too often at the expense of quality and customer service. We're not making what the customer wants; we're making whatever keeps those utilization statistics up there. And aren't we likely to overlook a few defects that might slow production?

-All the traditional performance methods encourage building inventory, the very thing we're trying to guard against.

If we over-absorb overhead, we have a positive variance and are rewarded. We've been duped into thinking that increased absorption means greater profit. What it means is more inventory, which has nothing to do with meeting the expectations of our customers!

We are now competing by how well we meet our customer's expectations. Our old methods of performance measurements were based on the assumption that we can sell as many as we can make. If we made a billion Chevys, then we could sell a billion Chevys. That is not the way the world currently operates. As one Detroit auto executive recently noted, everyone has to get used to living in a world where capacity exceeds demand.

We've been duped into thinking that increased absorption means greater profit.

The Right Yardstick

When we think of the performance measurement needs of the internal customer, it's useful to see it in terms of a pyramid.

At the top of the pyramid, at Tier One, are the top executives. There are only a few people up there, and their job is to monitor how the company is doing overall. They might look at five to six indicators, such as market share, gross margin, cash flow, earnings per share, earnings before interest and taxes, growth rate, return on sales, return on net assets or some combination of the above.

PERFORMANCE MEASUREMENTS

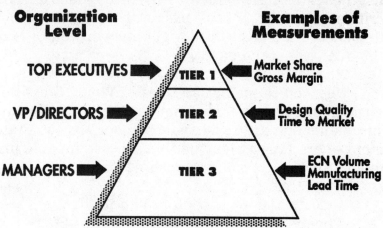

At Tier Two, we've got more people, maybe as many as 25 or more, looking at a whole different set of indicators—as many as 20 to 30 indicators, such as design quality, time-to-market, actual sales and production by product family, inventory levels, departmental expenses and budgets, productivity factors, new product sales as a percentage of total sales, inventory turns, warranty claims, etc.

At the next tier down, we've got managers (some who wear ties, and some who don't—key workers), and they're trying to keep tabs on hundreds of indicators such as manufacturing lead times, process variability, inventory accuracy, bill of material accuracy, engineering changes, product mix forecasts, on-time performance in Engineering, order-entry and Manufacturing, changeover/set-up times, rejects—all the nitty gritty of running a manufacturing business.

In the old paradigm, what we measured on Tier Three or Tier Two didn't necessarily contribute to improving Tier One's performance. Time-To-Market has a critical effect on market share. Yet a focus at Tier Two on Engineering expense budgets might cause a cutback of engineers and costs, with a resulting longer Time-To-Market. A focus on high utilization at Tier Two torpedoed the cash flow. In other words, we often failed to understand the relationships between the three tiers.

In order for us to forge a new paradigm, we need to go back to a principle of variability—measure the critical parameters. The basis for the new paradigm is to measure the right things. The new emphasis is on the quality, not the quantity, of the jobs done.

What are the right things?

We need to look at a series of World Class performance measurements, that is, performance measurements that are consistent with our Mission Statement—becoming a high quality, low cost, flexible producer. Such a list could (and should) include:

-Lead time reduction
-Quality of data, schedules and product
-Timely delivery
-Changeover time reduction
-Conversion cost reduction
-Actual demand versus forecast
-New products' percentage of total sales
-Volume of engineering changes

The basis for the new paradigm is to measure the right things.

The above World Class performance measurements also tend to have a profound effect on the Sales Department. People in manufacturing tend to look at the Sales Department with a mixture, to borrow a phrase, of fear and loathing. We've allowed ourselves to get trapped in a loop—the Sales Department sets sales quotas intentionally low, since they're paid a bonus for exceeding the quota. Manufacturing disregards the sales projections, takes what Sales sold last, then subtracts a few for good measure. Everyone figures everyone else is lying.

The result is that Manufacturing really doesn't have any idea how many to make, and Sales doesn't really have any idea of how many manufacturing will make.

Sales should be rewarded for sticking to the plan, not exceeding it and surprising Manufacturing. The same holds true for the plant floor, where the labor standards were often set at 80 percent of the true expectations, so we could exceed them and feel good.

The whole question of incentives, in fact, is a smokescreen. We say that incentives for exceeding the plan are necessary; that if instead, we reward for achieving the plan, people will sandbag.

They're sandbagging now. What we've done is abdicate the management responsibility to the performance measurement system.

It all goes back to our snapshot of reality. How do people really get paid?

We contend that if people participate in the creation of the plan and, in turn, understand the significance of the plan, then they'll tend to meet it!

Let's go back to our pyramid concept. The executives at the top of the pyramid have a responsibility to those on the tiers below.

1) The top level needs to understand how to read the instruments; that is, they need to understand the fundamental relationships between Tier One, Tier Two and Tier Three.

2) They need to make sure that understanding are in place throughout the pyramid.

3) They need to make sure the tools are available to meet established levels of performance and continually improve.

4) They need to frequently audit the process to ensure that the proper tools and understanding are in place, the correct data is being measured and conformance to performance expectations is taking place.

5) They need to make sure the measurements are being used to identify problems and take corrective action—not used as threats or punishment.

Accounting Issues

Realistically, we have to interface with the real world. There is no more rock-solid vision of the old paradigm than the tax authorities and the Securities and Exchange Commission. They demand certain financial items; theirs is not a negotiable request. Originally cost accounting was set up to fulfill those external customer's expectations, especially in the issue of valuing inventory.

It's easy to hammer the Accounting Department for performance under the old paradigm. Yet the Ac-

The Accounting Department only gave people what they asked for.

counting Department only gave people what they asked for—no more, no less. It did what it interpreted to be correct; collected what data it could and tried to balance the needs of the internal customers with the needs of those powerhouse external customers. When the manufacturing operations and processes such as planning, scheduling, plant layout, and so forth, were not correct or not well-defined, the "expectations" were not clear. The corresponding performance measures were not well defined.

More and more we are seeing companies that have different ways of assembling data for external reporting versus internal operations.

"The global competitor can no longer expect cost systems that only do a good job of valuing inventory to also provide adequate information to properly manage all aspects of the business," says Dan Owens. "Most likely, no one system can satisfy all the requirements."

Robert Kaplan is even blunter:

"You have to understand that there are really two types of accounting," he told *Inc.* magazine. There is financial accounting, which is what companies do for shareholders, creditors, tax authorities and the like...More important now is that managers are adopting those financial statements and using them to make important decisions about their companies. And for that purpose, the statements are fatally flawed."

The financial folks are victims of a Catch-22. We need to recognize the differences in needs for external reporting requirements and operating decisions, and that can mean keeping two—or even three—sets of books. This may be absolutely necessary to compete at World Class levels.

Who's Doing What?

There are two other pieces under the management accounting umbrella that we need to look at.

The first is the whole concept of tracking direct labor. Tracking direct labor grew out of the scientific management theories of Frederick W. Taylor at the end of the nineteenth century. What Taylor advocated

Most likely, no one system can satisfy all the requirements.

was looking at direct labor activities with an eye toward making them more efficient—the "one best way."

So far, so good.

This led to the creation of standards for measuring and reducing labor. Taylor saw the standards as a way to minimize labor. The financial people, however, saw the standards as a way to track—and manipulate—the financial health of the company. We began looking more closely at direct labor, breaking activities down into more and more detail.

A company we work with utilizes four work centers with a total of 16 operations to create a certain product. All 16 operations are done quickly, in less than a day, and the total amount of direct labor time is two hours, or, with an average hourly rate of $9 per hour, $18 in direct labor cost.

Management, of course, wants maximum control over costs, which traditionally gets translated as more detailed standard-to-actual variance labor comparisons. Which dovetails nicely with Industrial Engineering's push for more feedback for efficiency evaluations.

With the latest in high-tech data collection devices, each operation reports actual time. So we have sixteen collection points to keep track of $18 worth of labor!

We can collect this data, but each one of those collection points costs money. In fact, collecting any data costs money. Let's go back to our quality paradigm. What do our customers expect? What do the internal customers who need to use this data expect? Is it more than they need?

In another example, after close examination, a company found 283 employees spending a total of 206 hours a day in reporting direct labor transactions—enough to hire 26 additional people!

Do these detailed data collections add value to the product?

We may need the data, but in that detail? Does it really take 16 data collection points to keep tabs on $18 worth of direct labor? Are 206 hours a day to collect direct labor transactions worthwhile?

Think of the activity of answering the phone. Touch

Is it more than they need?

179

phone. Grasp with hand. Lift off receiver. Move phone toward face. Set phone on shoulder. Speak into phone. Cease speaking. Remove phone from shoulder. Move phone toward receiver. Replace on receiver. We could, no doubt, set up a series of standards for each of these activities, then measure how efficiently we move the phone toward our mouths. But why?

In a World Class environment, doesn't it make more sense to have an activity—answer phone, for example—and all the cost associated with that activity, including the direct labor, be billed to that activity? And modern manufacturing is much like answering the phone. Given the cost of the phone and the cost of leasing the line, the actual "cost" of the direct labor in lifting the phone and bringing it to your mouth is very small.

Cost manage- ment is the avoidance of cost. Cost accounting is the collection of cost.

There is, however, a valid need for information, with an objective of minimizing or even eliminating costs. That's cost management, the avoidance of cost. What we usually think of as cost accounting is the collection of cost. Of course, we need to monitor activities to assist in cost management. The question is how much detail do we really need?

What's happened is that for the first time in the history of manufacturing, we can collect virtually unlimited amounts of data. Previously, our desire for data vastly outstripped our ability to collect it. Now, with high-tech collection devices and the all-pervasiveness of the computer, we can collect all the data we want. But what do we need?

The additional challenge becomes how to collect the information we need without handcuffing ourselves to an outmoded system in the process. We don't want to be doing the wrong things better!

"We have begun switching away from our focus on direct labor control and moving to what we call 'conversion costs,'" says Dan Owens.

Fisher Controls defines conversion cost as those costs that can be assigned to and directly controlled at the manufacturing center or work cell. Examples include direct and indirect labor (although Fisher no longer makes the distinction), supplies, tooling, maintenance, energy, supervision, scrap and depreciation.

"With our new focus on conversion costs," Owens says, "we are asking the cost center manager to be responsible only for those costs he can influence. As it turns out, that's a pretty large portion of the cost pool related to converting products to their finished state."

Plant floor managers no longer have to worry about allocations over which they have no control, and office or general management can focus its attention on cost control in the remaining overhead areas.

"We feel that focus on cost control is the first step in cost reduction," adds Owens. "We can now provide the cell manager with meaningful targets that can have performance tracked against them."

How Much Does It Cost, Really?

One of the key areas in financial accounting has been the issue of overhead allocation.

In the existing paradigm, companies have allocated overhead costs as directly proportional to direct labor cost. Decades ago, this made perfect sense. For most of America's manufacturing history, direct labor made up the largest proportion of a product's cost. And, in the earliest manufacturing companies, which produced a single product—say, a textile mill making one type of cloth—overhead allocation wasn't a problem. The one product basically absorbed all the overhead. As long as direct labor remained a major portion of product cost, and the product line didn't become too diverse, direct labor is as good a way as any to allocate overhead.

The problem comes as direct labor shrinks. Manufacturing companies moved to increasingly varied product lines, and deciding how to assign expenses to specific products became even more difficult. Think of a completely automated factory—no direct labor at all! Try dividing a million bucks of overhead by zero!

Well, why should we worry? Suppose our overhead allocation method isn't perfect, how important is it?

In a World Class environment, flexibility is ev-

Deciding how to assign expenses to specific products added even more difficulty.

erything. In a World Class environment, we are react-
ing constantly to the customers' expectations. That
means a constantly changing product mix and a constant
influx of new products to meet those expectations.

Overhead has a significant impact on product costs.

We may be making our resource allocation decisions in the dark. We might be shifting sales promotion
efforts or engineering redesign to a product that, in
fact, is really less profitable.

In addition, as we reorganize factories into a more
process flow, the traditional distinctions between direct labor and indirect labor blur. For example, a
single worker might operate a machine, move materials, do preventive maintenance and keep the work
area clean (a way of working, by the way, that's already
common in some process industries). Traditionally, we
thought of machinists, packaging machine operators,
etc. as direct labor. Materials handlers, inspectors and
maintenance personnel are indirect labor. The overhead pool included indirect labor, plus engineers,
technicians, purchasing personnel, supplies, utilities
and tooling.

Overhead, too often, is like death and taxes—an
unpleasant necessity. What we've done, though, is
create this huge wastebasket, a slush fund, called
overhead, where we throw not only everything we can't
figure out where else to put, but a lot of things that
we've always considered overhead.

Again, we've created a couple of unexpected results:

-Because the people responsible for costs are
usually uncertain about what's included in overhead
and not involved in the allocation formula, they're
suspicious of the overhead cost assigned to them.
There's no assigned accountability, and without accountability, there's no control. No one feels any
ownership for the costs.

-Because we tend to think of overhead as fixed
and inevitable, kind of like a mountain, we don't give
it the kind of attention it deserves. After all, it's
everybody's problem, and that means no one's problem.
Overhead, then, becomes a hiding place for all sorts of

As we reorganize factories. . . the traditional distinctions between direct labor and indirect labor blur.

non-value-adding activities.

Before we look at alternative ways to allocate overhead, we should point out an important point: The real payoff is not in refining the allocation of overhead. Rather, it's in eliminating the non-value-adding activity itself. Isolating the actual expenses, not an arbitrary allocation, makes them more visible. Accountability for reducing those costs is much easier to accept. But the purpose is to minimize or eliminate the activity. That is the essence of the new paradigm.

Who Gets Charged For What

The simplest factory has one product and one group of people and equipment producing it. All costs are charged to the one product, and life is simple. When the business expands and many activities serve several masters, traditional methods of cost calculation break down.

Instead of the traditional method of overhead allocation, we need to move toward the concept of activity-based costing. Activity-based costing is a financial analyst's way of saying that the costs—all the costs—incurred in making a product should be assigned based on the activity or cost driver that generates the cost, including overhead and below the line costs, such as Sales, G&A, Research and Development, etc.

In the traditional paradigm, direct labor was the only, or, at best, the primary "activity"—the cost driver—considered and used to allocate overhead costs.

But is this a true reflection? What we want to see, remember, is that snapshot of reality. What is the true, total cost of producing the product?

What we want to do is break down all the costs above and below the line that go into the product, and charge those costs directly to the product. Without doing that, the cost of sales and the gross margin are correct by financial standards, but it may not tell us the true product cost.

Rather than arbitrarily charge all the overhead expenses by direct labor, for example, we want to strive to directly assign as many overhead costs as feasible.

The real payoff is not in refining the allocation of overhead.

Utilities, maintenance, supplies, tooling and the like are charged off as they are used rather than later as an arbitrary percentage of some overall figure. Special efforts in Engineering, Finance and Sales to handle special customer orders, all "below the line" expenses, need to be charged to those products using these services at a pro-rated basis. Look at the advantages to such a system:

-Ownership of expenses. The people who incur the costs are in the best position to control them.

-More accurate product costs. By directly charging previously allocated costs, we have a better handle on our true conversion cost; that is, the cost of converting raw materials and all other activities into product.

-More effective pricing analysis. By using an activity-based costing system to allocate overhead, we have more accurate product costs, which means we can more accurately analyze that product's contribution to our overall line.

-Minimized pooled expenses. If 80 percent of the previously allocated expenses are directly charged off—which is a realistic number—the issue of how to allocate the remaining 20 percent of the expenses is much less significant.

Driving Home

So how do we go about moving to an activity-based system?

One of the first things we need to do is to identify the cost drivers. Cost drivers are exactly what the name implies—activities that, when initiated, create costs. There are the obvious drivers, such as the activity itself. When we use the drill press to punch holes on sheet metal or turn on the blending machine to mix intermediates, we incur costs.

There are other not-so-obvious cost drivers, though. Engineering changes, part numbers, process changes, schedule changes, material moves, labor reporting transactions, placing orders with suppliers and product options can all generate costs. Activity-based

> **By using an activity-based costing system, we have more accurate product costs.**

costing identifies all those drivers and takes them into account for product costing.

Notice something else about identifying the cost drivers. Once we have them visible, we can begin to challenge each one.

How many of the cost drivers are non-value-adding activities?

This visibility allows us to apply the analysis techniques of the quality movement and steadily hammer away at unnecessary costs that have traditionally been overlooked—or accepted as "necessary."

"In a traditional direct labor-based system, the product is the cost driver assumed to vary the utilization of support overhead," says Dan Owens of Fisher. "In the (new paradigm), costs are assigned to the unit that caused the transaction to be originated."

Many companies no longer even separate direct labor out as a category, instead folding it into overhead.

"It's such a small item on the expense sheet," says Thomas C. Sternad, controller for Beckman Instruments.

Justifying Capital Expenditures

A company wanted to purchase an expensive piece of machinery that would drastically reduce lead time, giving the company a much more competitive position in a tough global market. The machine would also result in quality improvement, as a result of less handling and potential operator error. The one new machine would also replace several older machines, needing only one setup and virtually no move or queue, increasing the company's manufacturing flexibility.

Sounds almost too good to be true, doesn't it?

Well, according to traditional accounting methods, it was too good to be true. Direct labor was going to be more expensive because of the requirement for a more skilled operator, and overhead would increase because of expensive tooling and fixtures. The actual run time per unit would be slightly longer, even though the elapsed time to produce the product would be less.

Traditional ROI calculations give no recognition

Many companies no longer even separate direct labor out as a category.

for improved throughput, increased quality or increased flexibility. According to the traditional return on investment analysis, the new machine was a bad buy. By World Class standards, the machine was an excellent buy.

In the electronics industry, surface mount technology is a good example of this ROI dilemma. Surface mount equipment is extremely expensive, but it may mean key additional product features are possible: increased flexibility, increased throughput and better quality. The companies that recognized these facts and opted for surface mount machinery found themselves in the lead of the competitive race.

Sometimes customer expectations mandate a change that can't be justified by traditional ROI methods. Intermec Corp. went to surface mount technology to help shrink the size of their bar coding reader units, which their market research had identified as a major customer expectation. Again, Intermec found themselves ahead of the pack, a critical position in a hot industry.

"Tailoring better systems to manage costs—rather than simply allocating them after the fact—demands a clear vision of a company's long-range strategy," read a strong editorial in *Business Week* recently.

That is true. Changing performance measurements and cost accounting systems has the potential to tear a company apart. Yet it is unnecessary. It's worth noting that when the CAM-I research cooperative was formed to address the accounting issues, the Japanese declined an invitation to join—they were already using a similar concept.

In order to keep performance measurements and accounting systems from becoming a millstone, we need to subject them to the same intense scrutiny we use on our manufacturing processes, and with the same eye toward continuous improvement. Questions on performance measurements and accounting systems are quality questions, and need to be dealt with accordingly.

Traditional ROI calculations gives no recognition for improved throughput, increased quality or increased flexibility.

DISCUSSION POINTS

1) What are the Tier One measurements, and are they clearly communicated in your organization?

2) Do Tier Two and Tier Three measurements directly support high performance measured at Tier One?

3) What are the Tier Two and Three measurements? Are realistic performance goals established, accountability assigned and results frequently reviewed?

4) Does everyone—top to bottom—understand the linkage between Tiers One, Two and Three? Are periodic audits performed and reported, and action taken to improve?

5) Are overhead costs allocated on convenient or realistic activities?

6) Are product costs reasonably accurate? If not, why not?

7) Are cost reduction efforts focused only on direct labor or manufacturing costs? How much detail reporting is done to collect actual direct labor?

8) Have costs been assigned to those accountable and do they accept the accountability? Discuss the concept of conversion costs.

9) Identify any performance measures such as machine utilization, low quotas or purchase price variance that detract from World Class performance. Discuss how to change them.

10) Are financial justifications based solely on ROI formulas or do they consider other elements as well?

187

CHAPTER 11

Shifting Paradigms Into High Gear

Feel Good, Inc., is the recognized leader in its industry, and the company's 800 employees are proud. They're already making a respectable nine percent after tax profit, but they recently decided to introduce some new concepts on how they run their business.

Everyone understood that education was critical, and, accordingly, the company allocated $25,000 for an Education Program, with the President himself issuing a memo pledging his support.

Feel Good sent four people to an MRP II class, two to a JIT workshop and three others to a Total Quality seminar. Each person returned to the company enthused and confident that he or she had finally found the answer. There was, however, lots of disagreement about which particular answer was the right one, lots of pointing in lots of different directions. The majority of the employees, who didn't go to any classes, were simply confused. They didn't understand why the changes were so important, and when they expressed concern about trying to do several concurrent projects and their job at the same time, management chided them for a "bad attitude."

A consultant was brought in to teach two all-day classes on two successive Saturdays. About 75 managers and supervisors, mostly from Manufacturing, attended.

The President made a brief speech on the first Saturday, but left early to work on the Annual Report. Most of the Vice Presidents couldn't attend the Saturday sessions—"We're already on board," they said. "We understand this stuff."

The Corporate Training Director taught additional sessions using two boxes full of videotapes. About 100

IMPLEMENTATION

OLD PARADIGM
- Mandate Change
- Top-Down Directives
- Education
- Project
- Acronym Focus

NEW PARADIGM
- Buy Into Change
- Empowerment
- Change Process
- Continuous Improvement
- Solve Problems

189

people, in groups of 50, attended three six-hour classes. Each class had six consecutive sessions—45 minute videotapes followed by 15 minutes of discussion, from 4 p.m. until 10 p.m. Doughnuts were served.

The Training Director was heartened that there were so few questions; most people couldn't figure out what the videotapes had to do with their jobs. "Didn't they just tell us we're unique?" someone murmured.

Thirty days later, the Education Program was completed and implementation was begun. Three years later, it was still business as usual.

No one in management could understand, then, why nothing changed.

While Feel Good, Inc., can, in good conscience, check "Education" off their "to-do" list, they didn't get the results they expected or wanted. What happened was they seriously underestimated the effort necessary to change the way they ran their business.

We've seen this scenario repeated so often that we think of it as the "norm" rather than the exception. After spending big bucks on hardware, software, robots, automation and other tangible assets, companies opt for shortcuts when it comes to education—the heart and soul of implementing change—and end up running their businesses the same as they've always run them.

While a few people are exposed to the hard facts—and, frankly, concepts that aren't that complicated—the organization is not poised and ready for change. Companies' sizeable investments become extremely underutilized.

Shifting paradigms takes more than intensive exposure to technical facts.

When we talk about shifting paradigms, we mean something even scarier. "A paradigm shift," wrote Joel Barker, "is a change to a new game, a new set of rules."

We need paradigms to help us see; to help us keep our world in perspective. Yet, when the old paradigms no longer work, we need to be able to take the next step, to shift our paradigms.

Why would someone be afraid to shift paradigms?

This is the question on which change—and our ability to compete successfully in the 1990s and beyond—hinges. If we know the questions, and we have the answers, what's standing in our way? Why aren't we, or can't we be, World Class?

Maybe World Class is a little bit too large a chunk to bite off and chew all at once. Instead, let's look at the pieces that make up the whole of World Class performance:

High-quality, low-cost, flexibility.

Let's focus down another level. What are the problems, or obstacles, in achieving each step of our Mission Statement of becoming a high-quality, low-cost, flexible producer?

Well, for high quality, we need to put the responsibility for quality back at the source. Remember, high quality is consistently conforming to expectations, and that means expectations need to be clearly defined. That's going to require communications with our people, and trust, and training. We don't want any separate inspection.

For low cost, we're going to need more single sources, smaller lot sizes and less supervision. We need on-time deliveries, which means valid schedules and accountability for meeting those schedules, which is going to require more communications. We need to cut work-in-process and tap the knowledge of our thinking workers without fear of layoffs, which is going to require trust.

Flexibility, as well, requires crosstraining, reducing job classifications, valid, visible capacity plans—which also require communications and trust.

In other words, the most basic necessities for achieving World Class performance, for achieving our Mission, are communications and trust.

Not computers, not automation, not new factories, new processes, new programs.

Paradigm shifts; changes in mindset.

The conventional wisdom—the old paradigm—is that people don't like to change. Is that really the case, though?

People like change—the cliche that variety is the

191

spice of life didn't come about because people were afraid to be adventuresome. Outside the work place, people are amazingly open to change. Travelling to different vacation spots every year; learning new skills, hobbies and sports; pushing, instead of conforming to, limits.

In the work place, though, a whole different set of problems emerges. People aren't afraid of change. Rather, people fear the unknown.

People fear the unknown.

"Implementation involves changing other people's behavior, and therefore it is a highly emotional activity," Stanford professor Harold J. Leavitt told Robert H. Waterman Jr. "Everything the social sciences know about changing behavior says that people change for emotional reasons far more than for rational reasons."

When we ask for a wholesale change in behavior, a paradigm shift, we trigger a series of seriously rooted fears, concerns and apprehensions:

-They don't understand how the new ideas are supposed to work. Too often, we've kept our people in the dark until the last minute, explaining little, if anything.

-They're not sure how the new ideas will work here. They're not confident. Newer does not necessarily mean better.

-They're comfortable with the status quo. In fact, they just got good at doing their job the old way, operating under the old rules.

-They have pride of ownership in doing things the old way.

-The new ideas might work, but what if they don't? Life might not get better; just a lot of effort to accomplish nothing.

-Top management won't support the new ideas.

-The new approaches are just the latest in a long line of bright ideas that never get implemented. Fads that come and go, the "Hula-Hoops" of manufacturing.

-Management has been telling them for years that theirs is a "unique" business. Now management is trying to sell a "canned" answer to the business' problems.

-What about their job? Suppose the new programs

work so well that there are layoffs or loss of job importance?

-They don't understand what all the fuss is about. No one has explained to them why we need such a drastic change.

-Finally, is it all worth it? What they see you asking for is, basically, a leap of faith.

"Practitioners of the old paradigm who choose to change to the new paradigm early," wrote Barker, "must do so as an act of faith rather than as the result of factual proof, because there will never be enough proof to be convincing in the early stages."

These are very real, very legitimate fears, concerns and apprehensions. If we don't overcome them, there's no chance of shifting paradigms.

How do we overcome these fears and concerns, then?

The traditional thinking was that we could educate them away. The term education, unfortunately, kicks up a lot of not necessarily good memories from our youth.

We have a certain paradigm of what education should be, based on our experiences in school. Under that paradigm, education is learning the facts, reciting the facts back on tests, then getting promoted to the next grade, where the process started again. Next semester, you can forget what you learned last semester, since those same questions won't be on the new semester's exam. Learn, recite, forget. And that works—when all you need are the facts. But for manufacturing in the 1990s and beyond, the facts alone aren't enough. We're looking for a change in culture, a fundamental shift in the way people do their jobs.

Too often, we get the facts then go back to business as usual. For example, look at the long-term campaign to convince people to wear seatbelts. The facts are very simple and incontrovertible: If you wear a seatbelt, you're much less likely to be injured or killed in a car wreck. Yet, after 30 years of steady public relations campaigns, billboards, radio and television advertising, even laws, a recent *USA Today* survey found that more than 50 percent of the American public still doesn't buckle up.

The problem is not the facts. The problem is the tricky mechanics of behavioral change.

When it comes to change, there is a normal distribution of attitudes:

ATTITUDES TOWARD CHANGE

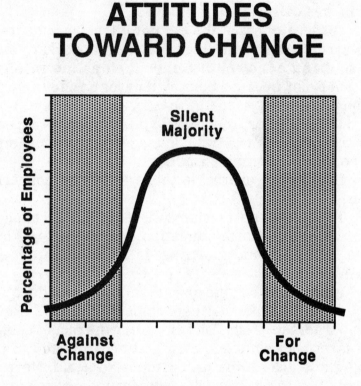

A small percentage, five percent or so, of the people are fanatics—they're the one's running down the hall shouting "MRP II is coming!" or burning incense in little Japanese shrines in their offices. They're the Rambos. We don't have to convince these folks—they're already confident, enthusiastic and ready to charge ahead.

Conversely, there's another small percentage, again five percent or so, who are equally confident. "It'll never work here," is their response, "and we'll make sure of it!"

But what about the other 90 percent? They attend all the meetings, attentively nod their heads 'yes' when asked whether they understand and are ready to pitch in. They shake their heads 'no' when asked if they have any questions or concerns. When the meetings are over, they go back to their jobs and keep on doing whatever they were doing before. It's business as usual. They don't hinder the new programs, but they don't help them, either. They're the Silent Majority, and if we can't swing them to our side, excite them about the new programs—that is, overcome their fears and concerns—the new ideas are destined for failure.

It's important to remember that the Silent Majority cuts across all departments and all levels of the company. There's an equal proportion of Silent Majority members in Engineering or Sales, not just on the shop floor.

Obviously, we can't go after the whole group, the whole Silent Majority, at once. What we want to do, though, is focus on a critical mass of people. An atomic explosion happens when enough radioactive material is packed into a dense enough ball to set off a chain reaction. That's exactly the plan here.

Management expert Peter Drucker has often pointed out that 20-30 percent of the population can influence the balance to change.

Who goes into the critical mass? We want to find the opinion makers, both formal and informal, at all levels of the company. Who are the opinion makers? We're not just talking about management and supervisory personnel. We're talking about people whose opinions are respected, people other employees listen to. Get them enthused and confident, and the others will follow.

"This battle of change," says Trane's Bruce Achenbach, "is won or lost at the water coolers."

It's important for the change process to give people a chance to express their fears, concerns and apprehensions. They need a forum to discuss how the new ideas apply, what the obstacles are to those new ideas and what the ultimate benefits will be. And it's their peers who are going to answer their questions and convince them of the importance of the new ideas. Mandatory education can't do that.

Instead of learn, recite, forget, our new drumbeat is learn, discuss, apply. There is, says Bob Stahl, one of

Our new drumbeat is learn, discuss, apply.

our associates and a longtime observer of the manu-facturing scene, a simple formula for change:

CHANGE = DISCONTENT with the present x VI-SION of the future x PATH of low risk

We need to recognize the problems with where we are, see where we need to be and have a high-confi-dence, low-risk path to get there. All three elements are necessary if we're going to effect change, shift paradigms. People need to feel discontent, that the winds of change are already blowing. In the world of manufacturing, even the most resolute ostrich must be starting to feel the breeze.

We must have a vision of where we want to be. That's why we've tried for specifics in this book. How much better can we be? Finally, we must have a path. If we're on a bicycle, discontented on one side of the Pacific Ocean, it does us little good to have a perfect vision of China. We need a path that shows us the way to reach our vision.

That's what we want to communicate first to our opinion makers, then to the Silent Majority as a whole. We want their understanding, then their enthusiastic acceptance, finally their whole-hearted buy-in, because that's the only way we're going to succeed.

A recent self-help book put forward an interesting hypothesis: "Everything I Need To Know, I Learned In Kindergarten."

There's a lot to be said for such a premise. But there are also some lessons that haven't served us so well.

One of the things we learned in kindergarten is projects. We got pages from the coloring book and a box of crayons; within the allotted time, we filled in the colors. It was a project. There was a specific be-ginning and a specific end.

As we progressed through school, the idea of projects became even more entrenched. We had science projects and English projects and math projects. We were taught to think in terms of projects, a series of specific events with a defined beginning and a defined ending.

There's nothing particularly wrong with that paradigm. If anything, it's one of the basic paradigms upon which much Western thinking is founded. We begin, strive hard, finish and are rewarded. Not surprisingly, we carried the project paradigm into our work place. So much so, in fact, that—as we've observed—we've overlooked the forest while becoming experts on trees.

Let's look at the by-products created by the project paradigm:

1) We focus on solutions before we understand the problems, implementing techniques or installing software instead of solving those root problems.

2) We delegate the implementation to a "project team," sort of the corporate equivalent of a police SWAT team.

3) We bring in outside "heavy hitters" to help the SWAT team out, like a real police department calling in the National Guard.

4) We expend our energies on such activities as fiddling with the organization chart, creating new Vice Presidencies to signal our "concern" for new programs.

5) We try to buy our way to World Class by purchasing new equipment or software and installing it.

There's nothing wrong with the project paradigm in many situations. Let's go back to an analogy of the family home we used a few chapters back. Building a new room on your home is a good project. It has a beginning and a clear-cut ending. Compare that project, though, to the overall upkeep and improvement of the house while you live in it. That is clearly not a project, although projects are certainly a part of it. Instead, there's a steady, on-going improvement process—correcting flaws, adding on, repairing and replacing.

People learn best if the information is in "bite-sized" chunks. If you set out to memorize every word in the dictionary, it's a lot easier if you take a couple of words a day instead of trying to memorize the whole thing overnight. And it's important to quickly apply the knowledge to make it stick.

People find it hard to open up to an outsider, whether that outsider is a consultant or the company "training director." People will open up to their peers, and that opening up process is critical to tamping down those fears of the unknown.

The Executive To-Do List

A great deal of patience is required.

All of this requires that, at the executive level, we have to budget both adequate time and adequate money if we expect to carry off these paradigm shifts. And a great deal of patience is required. The "quick-fix" mindset is simply not compatible with the change process. There are 10 critical issues executive management must address if we are to succeed:

1) **Get serious.** Make it clear how important these changes are and why. And bring the reasons down to a personal level—how the new paradigms will affect people's standard of living. There's also the element of excitement and competition. People love to compete, but they need to understand who the competition is and how it works. It's worth pointing out that Japanese corporations always consider their competition outside, not inside, the gate. Trane, for instance, posted its competitors' advertising on the company bulletin board and also sent representatives from the plant floor to major installations. The employees, in turn, began to see themselves in a global race, an "Olympics," where the competition was getting tougher every day. It's also important to set high goals—we can't talk about the Olympics and then call for a two percent increase in productivity. That's the old paradigm, business as usual. If you expect to win the Olympics, you've got to set World Class goals. The final aspect of Getting Serious is doing something.

"We consider implementation to be the last step in the process," wrote Robert Waterman in *Adhocracy*, "—something to be done by someone else...I've seen it happen again and again. First-rate people. Excellent analysis. Solid recommendations. Token implementation."

198

Clearly communicate that the decision to change is not a democratic one. It's not open to debate. Make the decision and get out of your chair.

2) **Face reality.** We have to see the way things really are. General Electric's CEO, Jack Welch, puts it best: "Face reality. Not as it was or wish it were."

This is probably the most difficult step—facing the ugly truth. When we look through the traditional paradigm lens, it's easy to think that we are doing well. Our schedules must be valid—after all, we're shipping product every month. We may be holding market share, we may even be showing one to two percent a year increases in our bottom line. Warranty claims are low, so we must have high quality. The fact is we've built informal systems to compensate and hide this ugly reality. We have to admit we have a problem—discontent with the present—before the change process can begin.

The most difficult step. . . facing the ugly truth.

3) **Create a change process.** We want to institutionalize change. We do not want to launch a project. Installing software or implementing a specific acronym is only a means to an end, not the end itself. The new paradigm has change as a way of life. We can't really predict what manufacturing in the year 2000 will be like, but we can say with certainty that, if you have institutionalized the change process, you will be ready for that world.

The function of the change process is to make Rambos out of the Silent Majority, and the quality of the process is measured by the level of enthusiasm and confidence among the troops. The change process takes time and is built around small group discussions, forums where people can openly discuss the new ideas, from problems to benefits. A key objective of this process is to break down the walls and barriers between departments, to bring new understanding to everyone involved. Shortcuts such as just sending two or three people off to a seminar or bringing in an outside expert to conduct an all-day session won't get the job done.

4) **Maintain a single focus.** It's necessary to break the acronym trap; avoid the fad of the month. There is always a quick fix, and the thing that ties all the quick fixes together is that they don't work. You focus on solving your business problems, on shifting from the old paradigms. We can't say it enough: We're talking about a journey, not a destination. This is not a project!

5) **Push ownership down deep.** Each decision must pass the ownership test. Whatever steps we are about to take, does it increase ownership for the new idea to the people ultimately responsible for implementing the new idea? When sportswriters asked members of the Detroit Pistons championship basketball team why their coach, Chuck Daly, was so successful, they unanimously answered, "Because he listens to us." No top down directives! There is no substitute for ownership and employee involvement. It is the only way we can solve those million $20-problems. The only way.

Each decision must pass the ownership test.

6) **Break the commitment stalemate.** The commitment stalemate—"Top management doesn't support the changes" versus "The employees won't get involved"— is a by-product of the old paradigm, strictly hierarchical management. In essence, we conditioned people to look to the Big Guy for the first move. There are two ways to attack the commitment stalemate. First, find out what the troops expect Executive Management to do to show commitment and do it. The second area of attack is to encourage action on their part.

Communications and understanding are the keys. When *Fortune* magazine asked Roger Smith, former chairman of GM what he wished he would have done differently, he responded, "I sure wish I'd done a better job of communicating with our people. I'd do that differently a second time around and make sure they understood and shared my vision for the company...If people understand the why, they'll work at it. Like I say, I never got that across. There we were charging up the hill right on schedule, and I looked behind me and saw that many people were still at the bottom, trying to decide whether to come along..."

7) **Lead by example.** In the words of the officer corps of one of the world's finest armies, "Follow me." If you ask your people to attend classes, you should attend as well. Even if you are already committed and have a good grasp of the new programs, your attendance at class still sends a powerful signal. People respond well to visible signals. As Robert Waterman says, "Actions are so loud, we can't hear your words." As one group told us, "We watch the feet, not the mouth."

Many of these traditional assumptions are left-overs from the 1950s and earlier, from days when we were just glad to have a job. Within the hierarchical business structure of the 1950s, the so-called IBM model, having consensus or buy-in wasn't really necessary. You did what the Big Guy told you to do.

And that wasn't perceived as bad or stupid. In fact, it wasn't anything out of the ordinary. Especially in a country coming out of a wartime economy. You always did what the Big Guy told you to do.

But this country went through a profound paradigm shift in the 1960s. While not delving too deeply into whatever baggage we carry with us from the Psychedelic Sixties, there is one clear and certain result: We no longer always do what the Big Guy tells us to do.

Our views on work and authority have dramatically changed. People are much less willing to respond to the answer, "Because I say so." From a worker's viewpoint, the new paradigm is, "Show me; convince me—don't order me."

That is not a bad attitude; that is a new paradigm. If you'd like, you can lament the passing of the Good Old Days all you want—that changes nothing. And, as in most paradigm shifts, more is gained than lost.

8) **Empower your people.** Where will we get enough bodies, enough people, enough human resources to carry out all these ambitious programs? We already have them. We need to give them the problem-solving tools, teach them the techniques, then turn them loose on the problems.

What we have gained with the new paradigm is

People respond well to visible signals.

access to all the brainpower of our employees that for years we'd ignored.

"Which would I rather have," Bruce Achenbach asks rhetorically, "me and a couple of guys sitting around the executive offices trying to solve our problems, or all 135 people who work here putting their heads together and coming up with answers? That's a 'no-brainer'."

At the Tennant Company, a task team was aimed at improving product quality. What that team discovered is worth noting. After nearly two years of work, the company-wide Quality Team identified the biggest potential problems for future quality improvements as...ineffective managers.

That included managers who did not know how to get their people involved in problem-solving and decision-making, managers who didn't know how to develop their people into skilled leaders, managers who didn't know how to teach by example, managers who didn't know how to develop an organizational climate conducive to solving problems and generating high performance, managers who relied on the old adversarial and autocratic style of management and managers who didn't know how to listen. Tennant corrected these problems and has achieved impressive operating results.

"The idea of liberation and empowerment of our work force is not enlightenment," says GE's Jack Welch. "It's a competitive necessity. When you look at the global arena, that's what our competitive advantage is!"

One of the most successful American companies, Motorola, spends about $44 million annually on employee education—2.4 percent of its payroll, twice that of an average company. The results? In one cellular phone operation, defects have dropped 400 percent in three years; the phones themselves have 70 percent fewer components and take four hours to assemble, versus 40 hours three years ago.

9) **Seek a constant catalyst.** When necessary, look outside for the expertise to keep the change process

going. This is where a consultant can be useful. Joel Barker points out that paradigm shifters are often outsiders without an intimate knowledge of the field— or a heavy investment in the status quo. Another important catalyst to change is cross-departmental task groups, what Waterman calls "adhocracy"—ad hoc groups or teams:

"Simply put," he wrote, "ad hoc organizational forms are the most powerful tools we have for effecting change. The clout of even the most aggressive chief executive pales by comparison."

Note the connection between ad hoc teams and Barker's observation on outsiders—by bringing together people from across the organizational chart and setting them on problems, we have created an organization of outsiders.

Look outside for the expertise to keep the change process going.

10) **Make it fun.** People respond to fun, to recognition, rewards and being a part of a winning team. That's why they're out there in the summer heat on the ball field or running that last mile in a marathon. People want to strive, to excel, and if we give them the opportunity to do that in their work place, they will go the distance. Phil Crosby speaks about creating a Zero Defects Day, and several businesses have similar "celebrations." Intermec stopped the plant for a party, complete with cake, when the first of a new line of printers came off the plant floor—the people who conceived, designed and manufactured that printer were proud. They deserved a party.

It's important to set goals, to have rewards and recognition. That's why the reach for "Class A" MRP II has proven so beneficial to so many companies. It's a clearly defined, measurable goal, worth big dollars to a company's bottom line.

"We were sending hundreds of people to the various training programs—MRP II, JIT, TQM, DRP, OPT, PM, etc.," says James N. Lyness of Eastman Kodak. "And then, without giving them any direction, expecting improvements to be made. Our people were confused, and we didn't obtain positive results until senior management decided to focus on 'Class A' MRP II."

It's a tough challenge to become Class A, but it helps put into place the teamwork and foundation that's going to be necessary for the rest of the World Class journey.

One of the most disheartening statistics we've seen came across our desk recently. It's from the Grant Thornton organization and, according to one of their recent surveys, two-thirds of the respondents said they had a productivity problem. More than half, though, considered the problem a minor one because it was caused by people, and the people could be replaced by machines.

It has always been one of the greatest ironies of American business that we're willing to spend millions of dollars in computers and software, literally billions of dollars in automation and yet balk at spending even a fraction of that number on our greatest single resource—our people. Had we spent one-thousandth of the money we tossed away on hardware in the last ten years on programs to make paradigm shifts a reality, we would have nothing to fear from the Japanese, the Pacific Rim, the European Economic Community, from anyone in the world.

Period.

A few years back, there was a popular song by the country group Alabama. The song was called "40-Hour Week," and in its refrain, a tribute to working people, was—and is—a lesson for everyone in manufacturing:

"For everyone who works behind the scene
With a spirit you can't replace with no machine
Hello America
Let me thank you for your time..."

DISCUSSION POINTS

1) Read the opening story about Feel Good, Inc.'s, education program. Identify the flaws in its program; discuss why they were flaws, and what should have been done differently.

2) Do you have a Silent Majority? If so, discuss why they are a Silent Majority.

3) Discuss the formula for change. Is the Vision clear, the Discontent unanimous and understood by everyone, and has a high-confidence Path been laid out?

4) Does the entire organization understand and believe that executive management is serious about changing how you run the business? If not, why not?

5) Is a change process in place to convert the Silent Majority into Rambos? What are the strengths and weaknesses with the process? How is the effectiveness of the process being measured?

6) Are the company's efforts focused on implementing acronyms, software and hardware, or solving business problems?

7) Who has the ownership for the changes being made? A select few? Outsiders? The entire organization? If anyone or any group has not taken ownership for their share, why not?

8) Is the entire organization convinced top management is truly committed to change how the business is run? If not, why not and what needs to be done to change the perception? Take a survey rather than depend on biased opinions.

9) Have you successfully spread ownership for making change throughout the organization or is it isolated to a select few? What changes are needed?

10) How are rewards and recognition being communicated? How frequently? Is there a general feeling that pursuing World Class performance is fun?

INDEX

Note: Several companies are used as examples extensively throughout the text. These companies include Bently Nevada, Fisher Controls, Intermec Corporation, Kodak Copy Products, Tone's, Inc. and Trane Company.

I

II

Also available from Dogwood Publishing...